I0425934

Court Approved Custody

This novel is a work of fiction based on a true story. Many of the names, characters, events, and locations have been changed or modified to protect the identity of the children and young adults depicted in this story and other characters my book is loosely based on. Names of certain adult characters within this novel are already in the public domain. Other than that, any resemblance to actual persons, living or deceased, outside of the confines of this novel is entirely coincidental.

Cover Design: CS Bennett /Model – Erika Tedder
Copyright © 2012
All Rights Reserved
ISBN-13: 978-1493782185

Chapter 1

It was dark and raining outside. A loud clap of thunder and bright flash of lightning unnerved my young frightened passenger.

"Where's my mommy?" five year old Tatiana asked me with a befuddled gaze as we drove to her foster care home for the first time. It was a question I struggled to answer for this precious young Shirley Temple lookalike. It was a question best answered by her parent for whom the child had been taken from. Professionals in the mental health field would say that it was a fifty-fifty proposition whether or not the mother would choose her daughter over her drug addiction if given that choice. Such was the state of the American family in today's drug riddled and family dysfunctional society. The fathers of these children fared no better. As a human, I remain hopeful. As a pragmatist, I am all too acquainted with the reality. "Oh God, please continue to bless the beast and the children….," I prayed.

As a caseworker in Florida's child protective services field I've seen more than my share of self-indulgence, recklessness, and irresponsibility by adults who considered themselves to be pretty decent parents. I've met people from all walks of life, some living less stellar lives than others, some surrounded by all of the opulence and material trappings we, as common people, usually fantasized about, and went after each week by way of our Lotto Fantasy Five and mega-power ball purchases. Some of us even believe that the rich have it made and have no reason to be troubled about anything. Nothing could be further from the truth.

On another level, I've met people who appeared comfortable living their lives on the edge. These were people who operated on the fringes of, or were either fully immersed in, what was usually considered unethical at best and illegal at worst. I'm talking car thieves, rip-off artists, bootleggers, gang bangers, shady hustlers, murderers, prostitutes, pimps and drug dealers. You see, some of the people in this category were parents too. And children were my business.

I've also met people of great faith and moral compass who lived and interpreted the Word of the Almighty in the strictest of terms yet meted out punishment as if they were gods themselves, children beware, I say. But if you think the wrath of God was something to fear, just try being a four year old child who found him or herself in the care of a full grown adult, an adult full of wrath and retribution. Ripped flesh, burn marks, and broken bones was usually the price that child paid for crossing them. Sometimes that child paid with his or her life.

The numbers were astronomical, the amount of children who suffered at the hands of adults and largely because of that parent's mental health issues and emotional instability. Many of these parents were so depressed and stressed out that they could only find comfort and relief in drugs, their minds lost in a chemical induced alternate world. On the reality end of things, their children were often left to fend for themselves or by others who did not always have their best interest at heart. Children who remained with parents who were mentally and emotionally afflicted in a way and manner that displayed maniacal intent, often found themselves in potentially dangerous situations with parents who were a danger to others, their children, as well as to themselves. Like lit firecrackers, they could explode at any given moment.

The common thread that connected these tragic lifestyles and social classes were the innocent children caught up in these dysfunctional environs, much like fallen autumn leaves drifting along the surface of a calm and serene brook until that brook merged with the whirlpool-like eddies of a rushing stream. Much like leaves, these unsettled souls were given little or no guidance by the powerful forces that held these children's fate in their hands. Where they ended up was anyone's guess, or so it seemed that way. As an underpaid, overworked, and often unappreciated caseworker, I knew that they'd often end up in a state run foster care home or in a relative or non-relative placement. That's where I came in.

My job was to protect the welfare of the children in my charge. But I was also responsible for providing their parents with professional services that would hopefully lead to the reunification of the parent and child, or children in some cases. In most instances it did. In other instances it just was not going to happen, for whatever reason. But workers like myself remained hopeful for a positive outcome in most of our cases. As for myself, I, Carl Samuel Benjamin, was dedicated to seeing that things worked out in the overall interest of the child and the parents.

When the child could not be returned to the parents, my job was to do what was in the best interest of the child. My job wasn't to determine whether or not the parent was going to be involved in the daily life of the child now or in the foreseeable future. That was always the parent's choice and the court's determination. But there were exceptions to the rule, for instance, my Doniella Bernacello case back in Palm Coast. This was a case where the child's mother, Maria, was deemed incapable of raising her daughter due to major health issues, including blindness, and not because of any neglect or abuse on her part. In either case, the child usually had no choice, or even a say, in the matter. With this, my story continues in St Augustine, Florida.

It was a little over a week since I was formally introduced to my new co-workers and staff members at the Family Integrity Program in St Augustine, Florida. My former co-worker in Flagler/Volusia County Community Based Care, Phoebe Coates, was present, as well, and was once again, my co-worker. It was because of her that I had applied for and interviewed for my current position as a child protective caseworker in St Augustine. It was because of the good word she had put in for me that I got the job.

St Augustine, known as the oldest city in America, was a favorite tourist trap for snowbirds from up north and people visiting from Europe before heading on to Orlando and a much larger tourist trap known as Disney World and Universal Studios. The historic district was architecturally reminiscent of its Spanish and Mediterranean heritage, though the British had a brief history in the area as well. One of its prized pieces of real estate was St George Street, which included several long blocks of shops and restaurants.

Located right in the center of this bustling tourist trap, St George Street was the major artery for those who owned mom and pop businesses and was a memorable getaway for tourists looking to experience a quiet subtropical vacation. But like most cities, St Augustine, considered one of the crowning jewels of St Johns County, had a dark side to it as well, though great effort had been made to keep its skeletons well-hidden.

Like every new city I arrived in to live or to work, I too, took in the main attractions but I also probed its dark past. A person could learn a lot about a city, or town, based on how it dealt with its scandals and its checkered past. In places like Rosewood, Florida, the town's history was so horrific that not only was there an attempt to hide the infamous event that happened there, the town was completely abandoned and destroyed. Events like this were never good for business, or a city's or state's image.

Notable in St Augustine's past were two little known but quite infamous events. One was the murder of former Broadway dancer and model Athalia Ponsell Lindsley on Jan. 23, 1974. That evening Athalia unlocked the back door of her house at 124 Marine St., placed a bag of groceries on the floor and walked out her front door to get her mail. Waiting for her was a man holding a sharp machete. Almost immediately he attacked her until she lost her balance and stumbled backwards. Standing over her, the man chopped at her eight more times, nearly severing her head. Months before her untimely death, she married former city commissioner and mayor, James "Jinx" Lindsley, who was a successful real estate agent. Athalia had social ties to the Kennedy family. The couple was prominent and the murder high-profiled. But who was her executioner and why did he want her dead?

An 18 year old neighbor fingered County Manager Alan Griffin Stanford Jr. as Athalia's attacker. Stanford and Athalia, though neighbors, had a running feud going on between them. Both were political rivals of sorts. When he was identified as a suspect, he claimed that county employees could verify that he was in his office at the time of the murder. But blood droplets were found in his county vehicle, a Chevrolet Impala, and a blood trail led to the wall of his property from Athalia's steps.

Now, a county worker decided he was going to find the machete and get the $500 reward, so he headed over to a nearby marsh, on foot, at the south end of Riberia Street at low tide. After a while he found a pair of trousers, a dress shirt, a belt, a pair of shoes, a machete, a baby diaper and a watch. The blood was too degraded to match it to Athalia, but the watch belonged to Stanford. And prosecutors noted that Stanford bought a new pair of shoes on the day they buried Ms. Ponsell. Because of shoddy police work and tainted evidence, the accuser was never convicted and eventually moved to Jacksonville, the tragic events of that day possibly remaining a mystery and forever.

The other dark event in the city's history was the story of St. Johns County's only known serial killer, William Darrell Lindsey. In 1998, Lindsey admitted to six murders in Florida and one in North Carolina. His killing frenzy lasted for years and in the late 1980s and early 1990s paralyzed the county. Only by several bizarre accidents of fate was he discovered, arrested, interrogated and imprisoned. Lindsey left bodies in many familiar local places, at the boat ramp in St. Augustine South, under the State Road 312 Bridge, in a pond on city property, and in woods near Hastings. Two of the women's bodies were never found. All of the victims were from the St. Augustine area. Some of the women were prostitutes and some were drug users. As big a story as this was, few living in the city limits can tell you anything about it. Those who could weren't talking. It just wasn't good for business. Far more have never even heard of the serial killings.

So what did these nefarious crimes have to do with my line of work? On the surface, nothing at all. But when one probed deeper, it became apparent that some things just never changed. Crime was one of them, abuse was another. Throughout the annals of time, crime has always impacted lives across the spectrum of one's social class, religious beliefs, and culture. In my line of work it was no different. Child endangerment, child neglect, child abuse, and child abandonment, like most crimes, happened at all levels of society and impacted all ethnic groups.

As noted above, both the poor and the affluent were capable of hideous acts of violence against their fellow human being. My point is that child abuse cases poured in from affluent family home settings as well as from low income family settings. Regardless of social class or status, such home settings were broken, at best, and dysfunctional, at worst. Someone in these homes was behaving less than what you'd expect from a loving and caring adult when it came to children and the abuse of them.

Often times the perpetrators of these crimes hailed from broken homes themselves, as children. Many came up through the foster care system, those from affluent homes as well as from broken homes. There were many victims as children but that was never a reason to become a perpetrator as an adult. Frequent victims of violent sexual crimes were young girls who had run away from home or from foster care. These lost souls often found themselves caught up in, or lost in, a very frightening and unforgiving underworld of prostitution and what was known as the human slave trade. Abandoned children fared no better.

As for boys, many of them were young runaways who found themselves behind bars after getting caught committing petty crimes and some far more serious felony crimes, like serial killer William Darrell Lindsey who was orphaned in infancy. You see, Lindsey constantly endured verbal abuse from his adoptive mother, creating a warped and violent psycho-sexual behavioral pattern that resulted in more than one failed marriage and an alter ego he called "Bad Bill".

Sadly, many runaways and abandoned children become what we'd classified as feral children, children left to raise themselves on the unforgiving streets of America. Such children could be found in cities in third world countries and abundantly. Rio de Janeiro topped the list of feral children in most studies. But it happened here in the United States too.

What made the cases I worked with just as notable, though they did not have the notoriety of the crimes mentioned above, was the sheer number of troubled children impacted by broken homes, some finding themselves at the mercy of parents who were troubled themselves. More common were children who hailed from homes that had at least one parent who was a chronic substance abuser or an alcoholic. Unlike the more infamous crimes mentioned above, the number of children placed in foster care never made front page news unless it involved a tragic death or some gut wrenching abuse was associated with the story. Like children who were told that they should be seen, not heard, politicians and business interests felt it necessary to keep such skeletons out of the public eye.

Yes, even in historic St Augustine, displaced children have remained, to this day, swept under the rug right along with the city's other dark and nefarious skeletons. But where you found people, you found crime. And where there were children, there was child abuse. Detroit, Philadelphia, Los Angeles, Memphis, Beverly Hills, Ponte Vedra, San Diego, West Palm Beach and Hyannis Port, the zip code did not matter. There was abuse going on and big time behind someone's closed doors. In this sense, St Augustine was no different than any other city.

Ít had been less than a month since the agency had moved into its new facility inside of the St Johns County Health Department Building complex and occupying a wing facing US1. The actual office area was located just across the lobby from the county's mental health department. New equipment was still arriving by the day. My desk, rather cubicle, was located across and forward of my good friend Phoebe's. The office area had space for up to ten caseworkers. However, we only had eight acting caseworkers. Some caseworkers had been assigned to work in areas that had little to do with casework but was still associated with the job. The eight of us, caseworkers who were on the front lines, were divided into two teams and each team was headed by a team leader. My team leader was named Tyrone Parrish. The other team leader was named Heather McKenna. Both were laidback managers and best of all, neither one of them were micro-managers. Of the original caseworkers, regardless of where they assigned to, whose names I had committed to memory, there was Elizabeth, Kristen, Tara, Mike, Myra, Allyson, Richard, Fred, Jamie, Rory, and of course, Phoebe. I was already well acquainted with Elizabeth since she oversaw two of my courtesy supervisions in St Augustine when I worked out of Bunnell, Florida. There was also Schquana, Linda, Laura, Jane, Sherrie, Sandra, Erin, and Raechel on the clerical and administrative side. Mrs. Joanne Johnston was the program manager. She was a highly intelligent and unassuming leader. She had poise and a calm that rivaled mine, I thought. And she was far more attractive and prettier than either I or Muhammad Ali could ever hope to be. Such leaders were rare in any field. A woman in control of her emotions, never once did I hear her raise her voice in anger. She was always civil with her caseworkers and with anyone else. Better yet, she too, was not a micro manager. All in all, she was the consummate leader.

In general, all of the caseworkers seemed to know their responsibilities and only sought guidance from the two team leaders for policy matters and special case problems. Other than that, caseworkers were given full latitude to be the professionals that our name Social Worker Professional implied. With this current staff and management, I had no doubt that I would thrive in this environment, even excel. Down the line there was even the possibility of a promotion.

During my first week on the job, I was assigned 18 cases right off the bat. Wanting to get on top of things right away, I spent my first three days at my desk reviewing each case and getting familiar with the names and issues I came across in the case files. I also took this time to determine what case needed a Judicial Review done, what case had a PDS (Predisposition Study) that was due, what children were missing a complete EPSDT health and developmental assessment, something that was required within 30 days of a child entering the foster care system, who needed a case plan drawn up, what case needed an ICPC (Interstate Compact) initiated, who needed a child care referral or relative caregiver funds, and who needed a referral for this or for that and in the immediate future.

By the end of day one I was ready to go out and meet with some of the families I had only read about. For me, it was like reading an interesting novel, one full of interesting and sometimes flaky characters, and a lot of them with quite a few twists and turns in the main plot. Where this differed from the characters I read about in such books, I actually got to go out and interact with the people I read about in the case files. Not only that, in many ways, I was expected to have a positive impact on these people.

The first family I'd meet would be the Browning family. The case involved seven children, who had been placed in the care of their paternal grandmother, two parents, both whom were currently incarcerated. The children were racially mixed. The father was Black and their mother White. The age of the children ranged from six to seventeen. All of their first names began with the same initial. As unfortunate a circumstance this was for the children already, their grandmother was battling terminal cancer.

Jotting the address down, I went online and searched MapQuest and printed out the directions. This was in the days before the widespread use of GPS systems.

Signing out, I got into my Cadillac and took off. I arrived at the trailer park some fifteen minutes later. And honestly, I was lost for words. Most mobile home parks in service had some semblance of a floral arrangement at the entrance into the park and some form of landscaping. Not this park. This was one of those throwbacks to the sixties and much earlier. The singlewides here looked deplorable and the property barely maintained. The grass looked like it had not been mowed in months. Low income failed to describe how bad this place looked.

Exiting my car, I found the singlewide I was in search of thanks to the description provided me by the grandmother. It was the first one on my left. Stepping up to the door, I knocked lightly.

Mrs. Browning, a widow, greeted me at the entrance with a warm pleasant smile. She was a tall Black woman with salt and pepper hair and pecan colored skin. She wore wire framed glasses. Her gaze was soft and gentle. Her overall personality appeared nothing short of genteel. It took only her introduction statement at the door for me to understand that this was a god fearing woman, and one with a positive outlook on life.

Following her lead, I entered the cramped space. A humble soul, and a proud one, she was almost apologetic about the poor condition of the home. The furniture was worn and the floor was in desperate need of repair. What remained of the vinyl floor covering was faded and worn. Several light fixtures were missing and loose wiring protruded from two wall receptacles which were also missing plate covers. In my estimate, the home was just as deplorable as the park it was located in. And to think that eight human beings lived here. On a more positive note, I knew that my agency was working on helping the family find and get into better housing, and hopefully one more adequate, more spacious, and more modern than this dump I found myself standing in now.

Because the current condition of the home did not meet safety requirements, the family had until the end of the following week to move out. So the agency would have to act quickly.

During my visit, I was introduced to four of the seven children. They were very friendly. All wore bushy unkempt hair, much like the afros of the seventies. The older three children were not at home; two teenage boys and their teenaged sister.

My visit was short since I was beginning to sense that Mrs. Browning was way beyond embarrassed by her current living situation and didn't want me to linger around too long. Frankly, I was anxious to get out of there. The stench, congestion, crawling cock roaches, and the dilapidated condition I found myself in were not conducive for a long visit. Before departing, I assured her that I would do all that I could to expedite the agency's efforts in finding her family a new place to move into and long before their current predicament became one of homelessness.

After bidding her a friendly goodbye, I returned to the caddy and jotted down my mileage and drove off. What I had witnessed was gut wrenching and quite sad. Why would two people come together, for whatever reason, and bring seven lovely children into the world and not be there for them in their greatest hour of need? That's what I pondered as I turned onto US1 and merged with lunchtime traffic as I headed back towards the office. I had planned on stopping at KFC on my return trip but after my eye opening experience, I decided to put off eating lunch for another hour or two.

I arrived at the office fifteen minutes later and conferred with my team leader Tyrone about the Browning family situation. Tyrone loved jazz music as much as I and he had a couple of CDs he'd love to play softly in the background as he worked. Today was no different. Playing in the background was a jazz tune by the late great jazz virtuoso, Miles Davis. A half-eaten tuna fish sandwich sat to the right of his keyboard. A 16 ounce drink was positioned to the far right of the sandwich.

As I conferred with him, he'd pause occasionally to take a healthy bite of his sandwich or a generous sip of his drink. In this business you learned how to eat and drink fast. Because of my agitated tone, which was usually mellow, he knew that I was beyond livid about this case. Perhaps it was little mystery why both parents were incarcerated. Neither one of them had ever demonstrated that they were fit for raising children, I told him. For these parents to have placed this responsibility on the back of a woman struggling to make it through the day with cancer eating away at her insides, they deserved to be where they were, I told Tyrone as I let off more steam. The condition of that house was deplorable and like none I had ever seen before. At least none that had people actually living in it. Well, there was one that was a little worse but that involved an elderly woman and another agency I once worked for. In that house I found weeks' worth of dried up dog feces on the floor and on the furniture. The smell was rancid, just outright sickening. Thankfully, the woman was placed in an assisted living facility for senior citizens shortly after my report on her deplorable living conditions.

After venting my frustration, I left Tyrone and returned to my desk to review my next case before I headed off to meet the family. The case name was Sergio Labriano, Jr. The three year old child had been placed with his maternal grandmother, Debbie Allen and her husband. The child's young teenaged mother was also in the home but she did not have custody or unsupervised visits with her son. The child's nineteen year old father, Sergio Labriano, Sr. was in and out of jail most of the time, mainly for violating his probation. He and the child's mother were no longer seeing one another, at least that was what we had been told. The maternal grandmother lived off of Riberia Street in the Lincolnville section of St Augustine, a predominantly Black area east of US1 and just south of King Street. The reason why we had a case on this family was because of domestic violence involving both parents. Mom was not granted custody or unsupervised visits because she had a history of going back to her child's father while under a court order not to.

Closing the case file, I leaned back in my chair and exhaled as I always did before heading out to meet the people I just read about. Rather solemnly, I'd relax and meditate and reflect on all of the pertinent issues in the case before I'd start thinking about possible solutions in hopes of moving the case forward towards reunification, and if not that, then permanency. You see, in this business, some parents took off from the starting gate, much like thoroughbred horses racing in the Kentucky Derby, trying their best to complete their case plan, and as soon as they could, so that they'd be reunited with their children. But others dragged the process out for one reason or another, sometimes for nearly a year. Some had legitimate obstacles in their way, but usually with some prodding and assistance by the caseworker, they could get the ball rolling again. This was not the case for all parents, though.

The bottom line, I'd tell the parents, was that whether or not they cooperated with the process, permanency for the child had to be met inside of a year, unless there were mitigating circumstances and an extension was granted. Otherwise, that parent would not regain custody of their child. Our hope, in the majority of our cases, was that permanency would be with the child's parent or parents. From what I had read, this case had been around for some time. That did not bode well for either parent.

Grabbing my clipboard and notepad, I signed out and headed for my car. It was a hot day outside and the caddy was just as hot inside, perhaps more so. June in Florida was always scorching hot.

My sentiment was right, I was reassured, the very moment I opened the car door and a blast of heat rushed my face. After a second or two, I entered the furnace. The first thing I did was lower all of the windows, then activated the cooling system.

Thankfully, I had a recent air-condition tune-up and in a matter of minutes the arctic-like air cooled the inside of my car to a comfortable level.

Rolling up the car windows, I buckled up and drove off to meet Sergio Labriano Jr. and his maternal grandmother, and possibly his mother. From what I had read in the case file, the child's mother worked and attended school.

As I headed over to Lincolnville, I listened to my favorite piano jazz CD and savored the drive. Lincolnville was a historic district and neighborhood that was predominantly Black. I loved visiting historic areas of interest. Actually, I enjoyed driving around all of St Augustine. Because of the tourist setting, I often felt like I was on vacation when I was out and about in the area. But quite often the cases I found myself involved with brought me back down to earth and a very stark reality, that all was not well behind some of these closed doors. What issues or adventures awaited me inside the home I set out to visit I could only speculate. Much like in law enforcement, when out on the beat, no two days were ever the same in my line of work.

Chapter 2

After missing my turn, and driving past the street, I spun my car around at the next intersection and doubled back. Turning right onto Bravo Street, I spotted the house. I parked the car across from the home on a street that dead ended at Bravo, the configuration much like the upper case letter T. Exiting the car, with clipboard, notepad, and ID in hand, I secured the caddy and approached the house. It was a two story stand-alone that was painted white. The house and street was separated by a narrow concrete sidewalk. Why they had a sidewalk on that block I could only guess because there was no one around using it. Urban improvement, I supposed.

I found the doorbell and rang it. After detecting no activity inside for several minutes, I decided to use the brass doorknocker. Soon, a head peered out of the second floor window. It was a young teenage girl.

"Hello, may I help you, sir?" she bellowed from above.

"Yes. I'm Mr. Benjamin from Family Integrity Program and I'm here to visit with Mrs. Allen and her grandson Sergio Labriano."

"Okay, she'll be right down," the girl quipped then disappeared inside of the window.

What seemed like a half hour later, there finally came movement behind the door. A hand opened it enough for me to pass through. It was the same young lady from the window who ushered me inside.

An inside wall faced the inside entrance which left us no choice but to make an abrupt left turn. After walking two paces, we stepped up, made an immediate right turn, and stepped up once again and entered into a large opened living room area. Mrs. Allen entered the room from the kitchen area.

"I take it you are Mr. Benjamin," she said in greeting as we approached one another and shook hands.

"That I am," I replied as I showed her my ID.

"You didn't have to show me that," she came back. "I remembered your voice from our phone conversations. You have a distinct and very deep voice," she added.

"Thank you," I said as she motioned for me to take a seat on the sofa. She sat down next to me.

"My daughter Alyson is at work and will not be here for another two hours," she began. "But little Sergio is here."

"I'll just have to meet with her the next time I stop by," I said, as I repositioned my clipboard and notepad on my lap. Scanning the space, I took note that the house was well furnished, clean, and comfortable. The teenage girl who had escorted me in left the room to go off into another area of the house.

"You have a lovely home," I said surveying the room a second time.

"Why, thank you," she replied in a gentle sweet southern accent.

The two of us talked about her daughter's case and about whether or not her daughter was ready to take custody of her son. Surprisingly, she did not think Alyson was ready and she hinted that her daughter was still seeing the child's father on the side.

"So, she seems more interested in the child's father than her son by what you're telling me," I said, jotting this all down on my notepad.

"Basically, that's what I'm saying," Mrs. Allen said. "Alyson doesn't think I know it but I have people who have told me they have seen the two together on a number of occasions."

"Well, when I talk to her, I'll reiterate that she has a set amount of time to get her case plan completed if she wants her son back. That's about all we can do.

"It all boils down to whether or not she wants hers child more than she wants the child's father," I explained. "Matter-of-fact, from what I understand, he was put back in jail just two days ago for violating his probation."

"That's what I have heard too," she said. "But I know she'll go and visit him."

I shook my head saying, "Some people just don't seem to get it."

"No, she doesn't get it because she's hardheaded," Mrs. Allen quipped as she stifled a cough. "Excuse me. I'm still trying to get over a cold."

"I understand," I said.

"Anyway, girls these days have little self-pride. God be my witness. I have talked with my daughter and I have prayed for my daughter and with my daughter in hopes that she will put her child first and leave that no good Negro alone."

"Hopefully, you will continue to hold out hope for her," I tossed in, glancing over at her.

"Oh, I'm going to keep on pray'n, that I'm going to do," she declared. "I know that my daughter will come around to her senses one day. I just hope it is soon."

"What is her goal in life or has she discussed this with you?" I asked.

"She wants to get into the nursing field," Mrs. Allen answered, grabbing a tissue and blowing her nose. "She works full time but she is going to school to be a nurse's assistant."

"Yes, I read about that in the case file. How close is she to finishing?" I asked.

"I think she has one more semester to go."

"Well, we'll see what happens," I said. "Perhaps she'll get her life straightened out by then."

"I hope you're right, Mr. Carl," she said. "Is it alright if I called you by your first name?"

"Sure," I said smiling. "I've been called a lot worse."

She chuckled.

"Hey Lil Sergio!" she called out as she looked in the direction of the kitchen area. "Come in here with grandma for a minute."

A split second later a little toddler appeared from the kitchen area through the entrance, which was shielded by a large cloth curtain that hung from above. Another young boy around the same age appeared seconds after him. Lil Sergio looked to be a healthy and spirited young toddler with a warm smile and a curious gaze as he scanned the area, his eyes settling on mine from time to time.

"This is Mr. Carl," she said to the boy. "He's going to come over and visit us from time to time to see how you are doing. Say hello for grandma to Mr. Carl."

After giving it some thought, and after getting a reassuring gaze from grandma, he looked at me, rather pensively, and said hello in a soft voice and in a very shy-like manner. All the while, he huddled close to his grandma.

He was wearing a short sleeve shirt and a diaper so his legs and arms were fully exposed. There were no bruises or any other markings that were evident. I then asked Mrs. Allen to show me around the house so that I could look at his sleeping quarters and the kitchen. She obliged me and took me on a tour of the house. I saw no safety violations or safety hazards and the kitchen cabinets and refrigerator were well stocked.

After my initial tour, I bid Mrs. Allen and Lil Sergio, as she affectionately called him, a good day and headed back to the office. Once there I settled in and entered my visit in the computer system.

Later, I made a call to the Florida United Methodist Children's Home in Enterprise, Florida. It was to be one of my last calls to my former teenaged client, Doniella Bernacello. I checked up on her from time to time, even after I left my job in Flagler/Volusia County, just to see how she was doing. We talked for about fifteen minutes. She seemed to be making the adjustment to her new caseworker, though she let me know that she still missed me and felt that I was the only worker who ever understood her and treated her like a person. I thanked her for the kind sentiment then bid her a good day as well. I would make probably one more call to her and then stop altogether. I felt that if she was going to bond with her new caseworker, if there was a chance for that, I would have to remove myself from the picture altogether. It sounded cold and indifferent on the surface but it was in the best interest for her to get past my departure. That was just the nature of my job.

The morning started off with a meeting with Mrs. Browning, her lovely adult daughter Brenda Tillman, two members of the Guardian ad Litem, my supervisor, and Mrs. Joanne Johnston, the program manager. We had assembled to talk with the family about how the agency was coming along in helping them find suitable housing. The agency had found a location the family could move into by the end of the week. We made it clear that we would pay the security deposit and a few other things, including getting the utilities turned on.

I made it known that I had completed all of the relative caregiver funds paperwork on the three grandchildren who had been placed with her more recently and that those funds would be kicking in sometime in the near future. She was already receiving relative caregiver funds for the younger four grandchildren. Understandably, Mrs. Browning was very gracious and beyond thankful. I was just as thankful. A person could only admire what this strong woman was going through in her efforts to raise seven grandchildren and battle cancer at the same time. I knew that her cancer treatments left her very weak at times. But her daughter Brenda visited her frequently to check on things and to help her out with the grands.

Once the others left, Mrs. Browning sat down. Her daughter Brenda sat in the chair next to her after smoothing out her trim, form fitting dress. She was in her early thirties, very attractive, and very married I could see by the gold ring she wore. She had her mother's warm pleasant smile.

"I want to thank you both for coming out today and I am just as thankful that we found a place for you all to move into," I began. "I'm going to deliver the deposit this afternoon after my agency cuts a check and turn it over to me."

"Praise the Lord," Mrs. Browning sighed with a smile. "You don't know how much this means to me."

"I'm just glad that we were able to help out," I replied.

"I imagine we can start moving my mother into the apartment after the main office gets the deposit," Brenda said, peering over at me softly through designer glasses.

"That's correct," I quipped. "Matter-of-fact, I'll call you Mrs. Browning to let you know that the apartment's main office got the check."

"Thank you," she said wearing that warm patented country smile of hers.

"Well, I imagine that's all for now," I said as I collected my things. "Everything seems to be in order. Do either one of you have any questions for me?"

"I just wanted to know if you're still going to be the caseworker on the case after my mother makes the move to the apartment complex," Brenda said gazing my way.

"Yes, I'll still be on the case," I answered.

"Good," she said, sounding relieved. "We did not care much for the last caseworker. She was nice and all, but she just did not seem to get too involved in helping my mother and my nieces and nephews."

"I cannot speak for that caseworker but I can promise you that I will do everything I possibly can to help your family members," I assured her.

"That's all we're asking," she came back with her mother's warm gaze.

"Okay, I guess I can say that our meeting is officially over," I blared as I made an attempt to stifle a yawn. "Please do excuse me. I'm still trying to wake up."

"Hey, that's alright," Mrs. Browning laughed. "At least God woke you up this morning. A lot of people didn't open their eyes to see this blessed day."

"That's so true," I said, rising up. "You all have a nice day."

"You too," Mrs. Browning replied, as she stood up.

"Nice meeting you," Brenda added, as rose up and extended her hand for me to shake.

"Nice meeting you too," I said with a warm smile.

That afternoon I received the rental deposit check for the Browning family and drove nearly eleven miles north on US1 to the apartment complex to deliver it by hand. I eventually discovered that the place was only two miles from the Duval County line, or what was better known as Jacksonville. Next to the complex was the Nease High School football field, the very field former Florida Gator and Heisman Trophy winner and NFL quarterback Tim Tebow played football.

To my surprise, the apartment complex was practically brand new. It had tropical landscaping at the gated entrance and manicured lawns throughout the development. Each housing section contained a three story building and a large lake sat behind the buildings. The main office had a beautiful lounge and game room area and even a computer lab. There was also a club house for hosting special gatherings. I was really pleased by what I saw, especially considering the dump the family was moving out of.

After I delivered the deposit check, I called Mrs. Browning to let her know the office had received the check. She was overjoyed to say the least. Getting into my caddy, I decided to call it a day and made my way home.

I spent the better part of the following morning in court. A very busy and hectic court session, it was a day clients and their attorneys and Guardian ad Litems and caseworkers mingled before, during, and after court. Sometimes in small groups and sometimes just one on one. Like most court hearings, it was long and drawn out. Only once in a while would there be some excitement, usually when the judge got fired up about something.

My supervisor Tyrone was present and a few other caseworkers. Slightly bald headed, Tyrone once served in the United States Army. He wore glasses and an affable smile. We seemed to see eye to eye on nearly everything. We were both around the same age, but I believed I was slightly older. Because we were both military veterans, he knew that I needed little supervision. And he knew that whatever questions or concerns I had I was wise enough to come to him with. Otherwise, he left me to my own devices. And that was fine with me. I never thrived under micro-managers. But alert laid back managers and I hit it off every time.

The man who commanded most of the attention that day in court was Judge Alexander, a no nonsense judge who had little patience, sympathy, or tolerance for parents who abused drugs. Child abusers were even lower on his list. Though he presided over his court with an iron fist, he was a fair and just civil servant. He could be quite pleasant and soft spoken, as well, but there were times he could be fiery in his delivery and was not beyond holding a person in contempt of court. I had known only one other judge who presided over her court room with such a forceful personality and iron-clad fist and I had stood humbly before a number of them with my clients. This particular judge presided over the Seventh Judicial Circuit Court in Daytona Beach. I remember one incident very well.

It was a hot summer afternoon in Daytona Beach in 2001. Inside of the court house things were heating up as well. As I sat waiting for any of my cases to be called, the presiding judge was addressing a troubled and defiant teenager who just did not seem to get along with the staff at his foster care group home. She was as stern and as forceful as I had ever seen her. After giving him a good dressing down, she was about to move onto the next case when the young lad, who was being led away by a foster care staff member, rolled his eyes and began mouthing off. Apparently, she overheard the boy's pronouncement that all of this was a joke and that she was nothing more than a tight ass *'bitch'*. When he said that, the stunned courtroom crowd grew as quiet as a funeral home audience during closing remarks.

Hearing this young man's high opinion of her, the judge immediately had the arrogant youth stopped in his tracks by a bailiff and returned to the front of the courtroom where she asked him to repeat what he had just mumbled aloud. He claimed he didn't say anything derogatory, which wasn't true because I heard him say it. Not buying his weak denial she had the boy, who didn't look so tough now, handcuffed and ushered into a waiting room until he could find it in himself to apologize to her and those present in the courtroom. It was either that or he was going to be held in contempt of court and jailed. Twenty minutes later a more humbled looking lad appeared before the judge, along with his attorney, and rendered a *mea culpa*. It was the most humbled apology I had heard in a long time.

After court, Tyrone and me, along with a few other caseworkers, went out to eat lunch at a seafood restaurant before returning to the office. It was one of those rare times we collectively dined out other when It was someone's birthday or baby shower.

Back at the office I met with Mrs. Johnston, just to update her on the Browning case and a few other things. After a while, we drifted into a conversation about a few personal things, mainly her family. Like most parents, she was very proud of her children and their accomplishments. I talked but said very little about my boring life outside of the job. There wasn't much for me to tell. But I did share a few things with her, including my interests in writing and in my family up in Philadelphia.

Matter of fact, I was leaving the following day for a one week trip up to Philly, something that was planned well ahead of my taking this job. Fortunately, the agency had no problem honoring my preplanned trip up north even though I was still in a probation period. She bid me farewell and off I went to work on a few case plans and judicial reviews. That afternoon I took off to conduct a few home visits.

After wrapping things up, I returned home and completed packing for my flight home. Early the following morning I arrived at the Jacksonville International Airport, parked my car in the parking garage, and made my way into the air terminal. By eight I was airborne.

Like most out of state visits, this one went by way too fast. I managed to spend time with my mother and other family members. It had been a while since I last visited with them. I'm talking years. While in the city, I bought my share of Philly cheesesteaks, soft pretzels, and Italian hoagies. I must have gained at least four pounds during my brief visit there. I even got to chance to ride over to Atlantic City, which was now considered America's number two gambling and adult entertainment spot, and hang out at a casino with a childhood friend and his father and uncle.

I returned to Florida and to work Monday a week later and to my utter surprise, I was told that Mrs. Joanne Johnston had resigned during my absence. I was stunned and totally lost for words. Little verifiable reason was given but the rumor mill was awash in speculation. The number one reason, and prevailing rumor, was that she got tired of being micro-managed by those above her. The loss was a significant one for me because her style of management, her engaging personality, and her professionalism was what attracted me to the organization to begin with. It did not hurt that she was attractive, intelligent, and had a charming disposition.

After making my way through the morning's disturbing news, Phoebe and I opted to talk about Mrs. Johnston's sudden departure over lunch. We decided on KFC just a block away. We took her car. Only once in a while would we eat a more leisurely lunch at an upscale diner because such places usually took longer to serve us and we usually had to eat our food and get back to the business at hand. Once seated, we began our discussion surrounding Mrs. Johnston's sudden and inexplicable departure.

"It makes no sense Mrs. Johnston had to leave," Phoebe began. "That woman knew the job better than anyone else and got along with all of the caseworkers. It just doesn't make sense that they found it necessary to micro-manage her."

"Who do you think was behind her leaving?" I asked, biting into a chicken breast. God, this was so delicious.

"I don't want to mention any names but it was probably her boss, the director of the program," Phoebe came back.

"Which one was her boss?" I asked, still unfamiliar with most of the upper echelon at the agency.

"The woman over mental health who wrote that book on mental health," she answered. "She's a little taller than I, white woman, kind of on the slim side, and she's got some gray in her hair."

"Oh, I think I know who you're talking about," I quipped, taking a second bite of chicken and savoring the flavor.

"There's no telling who is going to replace her," she said. "I just hope it's someone we can relate to and someone who can relate to us."

"I hope you're right, partner."

Phoebe took a sip of her soda by way of a straw, then said, "After what you and I went through in Daytona and Bunnell, we finally get a boss who is just perfect for the job and they chased her away. I just don't get it."

"It's sad, but sometimes it's like that Phoebe."

"Yeah, too many times it is," she murmured as she took another sip of her drink.

Chapter 3

While the agency went through a reorganization of sorts, even as I pondered the ramifications of all of these potential changes, life as a caseworker continued on. Thumbing through a checklist of things I needed to do, while seated at my desk, I felt a soft patting on my arm from just behind my cubicle. I moved my head to look in the direction where the patting came from. I didn't see anyone. Though befuddled, I returned to my work. Seconds later, I felt another pat on my arm. When I turned around again, a cute little girl stood just behind me with the biggest grin this side of the Mississippi River.

"Hello," I said, as I rotated in my swivel chair to face her. "And who might you be?"

"My name is Tabatha," she quipped. "What's your name?"

"I am Mr. Carl Benjamin."

"You have any candy, Mr. Carl?" she asked, obviously having already spotted my candy dish.

"I have some assorted mini Hershey chocolates," I answered, looking just beyond her to see who she was with.

"Tabatha, leave Mr. Carl alone," a voice at the desk in the cubicle behind me urged. "He has a lot of work to do and doesn't need to be interrupted."

"It's alright, Kristen," I said. "Is little Miss Tabatha allowed to have candy?"

"What do you have?" Kristen asked as she peered around her desk with baby blue eyes.

"I have some assorted mini Hershey chocolates," I answered back.

"Sure," she said. "Could I have one, too?"

"By all means," I told her. Taking the small bowl of chocolates in hand, I let Tabatha take a couple and then let Kristen get what she wanted.

"Thank you, Mr. Carl," the little princess said with a bright Shirley Temple smile.

"You're welcomed," I said in return.

"Thanks, Carl," Kristen added. "I just love these. They melt in your mouth."

"You're welcomed as well," I said as I swiveled my chair around and returned to my notes.

That evening I met with my friend and dining partner, Cynthia, and had dinner with her at Sonny's Barbeque Restaurant in Palatka, Florida. I had picked her up in East Palatka off of SR-207 where she lived on the way back from St Augustine. I ordered a combination chicken and rib dinner and she, her favorite, baby back ribs. After dinner, we went to a nearby carwash and vacuumed the inside of my car, then drove it into the wash bay where we soaped it down, scrubbed it clean, and then spray rinsed it. We did this from time to time whenever we got together. Usually we'd take both of our cars to the carwash and work on one, and then the other's car. Somehow before we finished, we'd both wound up getting wet, though I did my best not to wet her above her shoulders. Women were always complaining about getting their hair wet, for whatever reason. But we had fun.

After returning her home, I headed to Interlachen some 16 miles west of Palatka where my home was. I called my mother in Philly and talked with her briefly, relaxed a while, then I decided to return to work on my latest novel, another romance. With all of the time I had on my hands after work, I had taken to writing to pass the time away. Whether or not they were good enough stories to be published, I did not care at the time. I just loved writing. And like I said, it helped pass the time away.

*L*eaning back in my chair at my desk, the following day, with a thick file positioned on my lap, I went over a new case that had just been transferred to me from my coworker named Richard. It was the Eleanor Boatwright case. Richard had gone over a few things with me about the case but I wanted to delve a little deeper into it. The case involved a young mother in her mid-twenties and her two young boys. There were two fathers involved in the case but not in the boys' lives or in the mother's life. Neither one of them had ever shown up to court.

Both children had been placed in the care and custody of their maternal great aunt, Eleanor Kratz, whom they had lived with off and on in the past. The mother, who preferred to be called Penny, had been diagnosed as being bi-polar and unable to properly care for the children. It read in the case file that the children were often left to entertain and fend for themselves while mother slept or went out. Mother was also taking multiple medications, some, which were either over-prescribed or the mother had just decided to exceed the proper dosage. Mother had been granted supervised visits with the boys. A dropout, she attended First Coast Technical Institute's Career Navigators Program, just off of SR 16 on Collins Avenue in St Augustine.

Sometime that afternoon I'd head down to Flagler Estates, some eleven miles south of our office. Hopefully, I'd get to meet the great aunt, Eleanor Kratz, and the two young boys, Mason and Jason at her home. Hopefully, the boys' mother would be there, as well. It was an area and community of mainly manufactured homes and a few site-built homes, most which sat on at least an acre of land.

I was about to work on a judicial review report when my supervisor approached me.

"Hey Carl," he said abruptly. "I need you to run over and pick up one of Tara's children at his school. She's out on another case and they need the child picked up right away. He's in the principal's office."

"He has a medical appointment or something or is he sick?" I asked.

"Neither one," he replied. "He's been acting up in class and is said to have hit the teacher."

"How old is the kid?" I asked.

"Around six years old."

"Six!" I exclaimed. "You're kidding me."

"He's part of that six member family of children who are all problem kids in school and in foster care," Tyrone explained. "They're just defiant and out of control."

"Where do you want me to take him to?"

"Just bring him here," he said. "I'll keep an eye on him until Tara returns."

"Okay boss," I said. With that he gave me the name of the child, the school, and the principal's name, and instructions on how to find the school. Putting my files away, I took off.

The school was about four miles from our office but it involved a lot of twists and turns. I parked the caddy and found my way to the main office. I introduced myself to the staff and was escorted by one of them to the principal's office a short distance away.

The principal was a Black woman in her early forties and wore her age well. She was standing by her desk talking with someone on the phone when we entered her office. I am sure she had children but her shapely form did not hint of her having any at all. She dressed and conducted herself in a regal manner. After hanging up the phone, she approached me and gave me a warm friendly greeting, one professional to another. Sitting down on a chair in front of her desk was the six year old Tasmanian devil himself, Horatio Wallace. He seemed innocent enough as he sat there demurely and quietly. It was hard to fathom that this child was such a hellraiser. Hell, anyone over eighty pounds could have threatened to sit on a kid like this back in the day and he'd cry uncle. Kids these days would dare you to sit on them and talk trash while you considered doing exactly that. Hard headedness is what we called it years ago. Oppositional Defiant Disorder is what they called it today.

"Glad to meet you Mr. Benjamin. I'm Principal Geraldine Maxwell," she said, folding her arms in front of her and looking in the direction of Horatio. "Mr. Wallace here seems to think he can beat up on my teachers and his classmates. I've had a long talk with him and told him this sort of behavior will not be tolerated in my school. Now, because of his inappropriate behavior I've decided that he needs to take the rest of the day off."

"I understand this is not the first time he's been excused from school," I tossed in.

"No, it isn't" she replied. "He's been in trouble before. Look, can we step outside of my office for just a second and talk, Mr. Benjamin?"

"Sure," I answered.

Turning to her office assistance, she said, "Nancy, could you keep an eye on little Mr. Wallace here while I have a private chat with Mr. Benjamin?"

"No problem at all, Mrs. Maxwell," her office worker said before turning her gaze back on Horatio.

The principal and I left her office as she guided me out of Horatio's hearing range.

"I understand that you are not his caseworker but do you know if he's been taking his meds like he should?" she asked me. "Usually when he takes his meds his behavior is more in line with what we expect out of our children."

"I wished I had an answer for you on that but I have no clue what he's taking and if he's taking it as he should," I replied. "I would hope so, but I can have the assigned caseworker look into it when I see her."

"Please do," she asked. "I'm the new principal here and from what I know, this sort of behavior has been allowed to go on unchecked in the past. But like I told him, I am not going to tolerate kids hitting my teachers and staff members. Period."

"I understand," I said. "And if I were you I wouldn't tolerate it either."

"Please, I apologize if I've come off like I am upset with you or the assigned caseworker. I'm not," she said apologetically. "You all did not bring these children into the world and are not responsible for their behavior. I know you're doing the best that you can. I know that we are. But our hands are tied. I'm just expressing my personal frustration with these children's parents and a system that allow these children to think they can get away with acting out."

"I totally agree with you," I added. "When I worked in Daytona Beach, one of my coworkers had an eight year old in her caseload who was brought up on charges of stabbing a teacher with a pencil. The teacher's leg got infected and it put her out of work for two months."

"Oh no, that's not going to happen here, darling," she affirmed. "They'd have to fire me but if it came down to that, a child stabbing me, it's going to be lights out for that kid, I can assure you of that. They're not paying me enough to be assaulted."

"I feel the same way," I quipped. "Children these days have little or no respect for adults or any other authority. Yes, like you, I'd have to go to jail if I was threatened with bodily harm."

"Okaay," the principal sighed, clasping her hands just below her chin. "Listen, I know you are probably as busy as I am so I'm not going to hold you up any longer," she said, gazing up at me. "But it was good to meet you and hopefully Horatio will get his act together."

"I hope so," I replied as she led me back towards her office where I took custody of the child. I showed him my ID card and explained to him who I worked for and why I was there and where we were going. He seemed to already know where he was going. After all, he had been through this routine a number of times in the past.

I signed him out, and myself, and we headed outside and over to my car. I buckled him in the back seat and I got in and we took off. He was quiet throughout the ride. When I returned to the office, I turned him over to my supervisor, Tyrone.

"Had any problems with him on the way back?" he asked me.

"None at all," I answered. "He was quiet as a mouse."

"Good," he smiled. "You are pretty much a quiet guy but I know there are times you can give a child or anyone for that matter, that serious look and they know you mean business."

"Sometimes you have to get that across from the onset, that you mean business," I declared.

"Well, if that's what it takes to get the message across, more power to you. I'm for it," he smiled. "So what's on your agenda for the rest of the day?"

"Just judicial reviews to finish up and have you look over and sign off on."

"What case?"

"The Browning case."

"Whew!" Tyrone sighed. "I admire that grandmother for taking in all of those grandchildren of hers. I don't know if I could have done it."

"I know what you mean," I replied. "And we're not exactly talking about the Brady Bunch here either."

"You're right about that," he said, letting me know that he remembered that seventies television series.

"Well, good luck with Mr. Horatio here," I said peering over at the lad, who was thumbing through a children's book Tyrone had given him. "Tell Tara I'll fill her in on what the principal had to say to me when she returns."

"Will do," he said, as he picked up his phone to dial out.

"I'll talk to you later," I said.

"It's supposed to storm later so drive safely when you head out this afternoon, especially while driving on those back roads in Flagler Estates," he murmured as he turned his full attention to the voice at the other end of the phone.

"I will," I uttered softly.

Walking back to my desk, I dove into my paperwork and took a few phone calls. Around four that afternoon, I tidied up my cubicle area and signed out to Flagler Estates. A home visit was the stated reason.

Halfway into my drive it began to rain, just as Tyrone had predicted. I wasn't concerned about US1 and SR 11 but I was concerned about the rain coming down on the mainly dirt roads of Flagler Estates. The mud this rain could produce was the kind that would strand you if you did not have a four wheel drive vehicle. Not only that, some roads were adjacent to fifteen foot drop offs into ravines. Such roads, if they ever got slippery, could send you sliding over the edge and down into the ravine. If you had any speed when you went into a slide, it would be like driving over a cliff. It could get pretty dangerous there when it rained. And there were times when it was raining hard that I found myself creeping along slowly so that I would not lose control of my car and go into the ravine.

Thankfully, by the time I arrived at the estates, the rain had ceased and most of the roads had dried up from the sun and the summer heat. Using my MapQuest printout, I finally found the house and backed in on the driveway. The doublewide manufactured home was set back a good distance from the road.

Getting out of my car, with notepad and clipboard in hand, I approached a wooden fence that sealed off the rest of the property in close proximity of the house. The reason I could see right off the bat. She had at least four canines roaming about inside, two were very large dogs. The other two were small. As in most of the cases, it was the little ones who barked the loudest and the most constant. The larger two dogs barked every fifteen seconds or more, just to let their presence be known, then they'd turn and stroll off a short distance before returning with another announcement.

Without sounding alarming, I called out *'hello'* a few times as loud as I could above the barking dogs before the door to the home finally opened. A gray haired woman, who looked the role of grandma, peered over at me and smiled.

"Mr. Benjamin, no doubt," she said, exiting the door and stepping down the patio stairs.

"That's me," I answered. "And you're Mrs. Eleanor Kratz."

"Miss Eleanor Kratz," she corrected me, as she approached the fence.

By now all four dogs were howling like crazy.

"Oh, they won't bite you," she assured me as she opened the wooden gate. "Their bark is louder than their bite, as the saying goes," she chuckled.

On her word, I entered the inner sanctity of her property, a property guarded by these four four-legged creatures I was now supposed to suddenly trust. But true to her word, they did not bite. After I was inside, they quieted down. I must say that I breathed a sigh of relief having made it inside. Now it was time to get down to business.

Mason, the six year old, was up and walking about. Jason, the two year old was asleep in his crib. The home was plain but comfortable. She had ample furniture and lighting and I saw no visible signs of safety hazards.

"This is Mason," Miss Eleanor said as she introduced me to the youngster. "We call him Mace for short."

"Hello Mace," I said, extending my hand for him to shake. "My name is Mr. Carl Benjamin. You may call me Mr. Carl."

"Howdy Mr. Carl," he said laying five on my hand. "Are you a cop?"

"No, I am a caseworker," I said.

"What's a caseworker?" he asked.

"Someone who comes out and makes sure you are alright and someone who going to help your mother in a way so that you get to spend more time with her. Would you like that?"

"Yes," he answered unabashedly.

"Jason is in the bedroom, if you want to see him now," Miss Eleanor said.

"If he's asleep, I'll check in on him just before I'm ready to leave," I said. "Is Penny going to stop by today?"

"She said she would but knowing her, she probably will not."

"Do you know if she is still attending the vocational school up in St Augustine?"

"Yes. That I know she's doing. Everything else I have to guess long and hard about concerning her comings and goings."

"I see."

For the next fifteen minutes she filled me in on the issues she has had with her niece and her bout with prescription drugs. She gave me a history of Penny's involvement with the two fathers of her children. There had been domestic violence in all of her relationships I was told.

After she brought me up to speed on Penny I talked about what was needed in order for Penny to regain custody of her boys. This included her having stable housing, stable employment, and paying child support, along with both fathers, to the aunt until Penny was granted custody of them. She also needed to complete substance abuse classes, domestic violence classes, and age appropriate parenting classes, since she had a habit of treating her oldest son as more a little brother than her son. She also had anger management issues she needed to address and mental health counseling she needed to participate in. I assured Miss Kratz that the referrals for all of these services had already been submitted by me days earlier. All that was left for me to do was to meet and talk with Penny and in the near future, I told her.

Before leaving, I checked in on the youngest boy, Jason. I had the child's great aunt wake him up. Though one might think it needless to wake up a sleeping child, it was my job to make sure he could be awakened. That's why I always had a sleeping child or baby stirred awoke before I left a visit. Any sleeping child could be lying there comatose. People who abuse children are pretty crafty. Not knowing if I'd ever run into one, I made sure that I remained a step ahead of them.

Sensing that all was well in this household and with this caregiver, I departed. Next stop...home.

Chapter 4

Several days later, I decided I'd check in on Mrs. Browning to see how things were going in their new abode. After my court hearings that morning, I returned to the office and went over a few case reviews with my supervisor and then went off to lunch with Phoebe. We took her car again. We ate at Taco Bell just off of US1, a block or two from the office. While there we speculated who might take over Mrs. Johnston's position. Afterwards, we drove a mile north on US1 and stopped at a Dairy Queen so that she could purchase a cup of her favorite tasting coffee. Then we headed back to the office.

When I arrived at my desk, I got word that Penny Boatwright was waiting to see me. Going out to the lobby, which was located between our offices and the entrance to the mental health's office, I came to a stop and announced her name. Penny immediately stood up and approached me with a trace of a smile.

"Hello, I'm Carl Benjamin," I said introducing myself.

"I'm Penny Boatwright," she replied as we shook hands. She was a pretty young mother, with long brown hair and brown eyes, but in my estimate, she was far too young to be having children with the problems she was having with prescription drugs and men. But I would give her a chance to explain her side of the story since everyone else has had their say.

"Please, will you come with me," I said as I led her back into our area. I took her inside of a room where we could talk in confidence. Closing the door, we sat down across from one another. She was wearing a light colored blouse, dark skirt, and smoke colored nylons. It wasn't quite the picture I had of her. She seemed mature enough sitting there with her legs crossed, her hands clasped on her lap, and conducting herself in an adult manner. I was really expecting her to show up wearing jeans and braids and tattoos, the way she was described in the case file.

"So we finally meet," she said, beating me to the punch.

"Yes," I replied as I scratched my right shoulder briefly with my left hand. "I set out to meet with you and your family the other day but you were not there."

"Yeah, I heard. I wanted to stop by then but my friend who was supposed to pick me up had to pick up her son's father first and he worked at a mechanic shop that was just short of the Duval County line. So I never made it back in time to meet you. But my mom told me that you had stopped by."

"Your mom?" I asked curiously. "I thought Miss Eleanor Kratz was your aunt."

"She is, but I call her mom because she is like a mother to me."

"I see," I murmured, absorbing everything she said.

"So, you're going to be my caseworker now."

"Yes, I am," I replied.

"Good, my last caseworker and I did not see eye to eye on a lot of things," she said leaning forward. "You know something? I don't think he really cared for me as a person."

"Why would you say that?" I asked.

"Well, I've made some mistakes in my life and some people just look down on you because you have made mistakes. Besides, he and I often got into it because I told him that I did not abuse my prescriptions. I got the dosage wrong and that is why I almost OD."

"So, you're saying that you had a smaller dosage at one time and they increased it later and you forgot."

"Yes, before, I was taking two pills at a lower dosage, then they gave me a stronger prescription and I was only supposed to take one. I just happened to take one too many one morning and got real sick. My other caseworker never believed me."

"But that's what happened," I tossed in.

"That's exactly what happened," she replied sitting poised on the sofa chair.

"Well, this may surprise you but I too, once took the wrong dosage of medication. It was a pill that had some side effects I wasn't aware of because I never bothered to read the label. I didn't know it dehydrated me and depleted my potassium level. On top of that, I was supposed to take only one tablet but somehow I was thinking that I was supposed to take two. One hot summer day, when I was out and about, and had no breakfast and no fluids inside of me, I collapsed. I was so far gone that I was hospitalized for five days. So I know it can happen."

"Well, I am glad someone else knows what it is like to screw up like that," she said.

"Thankfully, I didn't die or was labeled a drug abuser."

"But I was, though I'm glad you didn't die either."

Penny and I went on to talk another fifteen minutes. After a while I realized that she had just made some bad choices in her life. She wasn't a bad person, just misguided. We talked about the men in her life and the domestic violence that was on record and it was all about a young woman who didn't take being abuse lightly and fought back, or as they say, she got even.

After that, we went over what she needed to get done on her case plan. She told me that she had attended the case plan conference just before I got the case, which I already knew, but I assured her that I had already put in the referrals she needed to get started. On the way out I asked her not to be so hard on my coworker. I'm sure their past clashes had more to do with their distinct personalities than anything else. She smiled and we bade one another goodbye. Taking the lead, I escorted her out into the main lobby.

An hour later I was on my way to visit Mrs. Browning and her grandchildren. I made the eleven mile trip in thirty minutes rather than in my usual twenty minutes due to heavy traffic.

Parking the caddy, I found my way to the unit. I depressed the doorbell button and waited for someone to answer the door. It wasn't long before the door opened and Mrs. Browning's smiling face appeared. She invited me inside but asked me to take my shoes off before proceeding into the main living room area. She said that the carpet was brand new and that she was afraid of it getting soiled and having to pay for it whenever the day came for them to move out. I had no problems taking my shoes off, I told her.

"So, how is everything so far?" I asked her as we sat at a table in the dining room area.

"Just fine," she beamed. "I am so happy to be here. But as you can see, there's hardly any furniture. Everyone has been sleeping on the carpet."

"Yes, I noticed that there's really no furniture, except for this table," I replied.

"My daughter gave us this table," she said, rubbing the side of her nose with her finger before slightly adjusting her glasses with the same finger. "But God is good. I talked to a local Christian charity the other day and told them about our situation and they are going to donate four beds and a suite of furniture. They're going to deliver them tomorrow."

"Well, you can't beat that," I quipped with a smile.

"You ready for a tour?" she asked me.

"Sure, why not," I smiled.

From one empty room to another we went as she showed me where the girls slept and the boys and her bedroom. It was a four bedroom apartment. The kitchen was modern with a dishwasher and garbage disposal. There was also a refrigerator and microwave oven.

The oldest girl and two younger children were present. Fanisha, the oldest girl, was sent to retrieve her brothers who were over at the computer lab at the main office. In a short while they all converged on the scene with smiles. For the next twenty minutes, I talked to them individually and as a group and conveyed upon them how essential it was for them to help their grandmother out and to keep as much stress off of her as possible.

Before leaving, I took aside Frederick, the oldest child, and led him outside where we sat down at the bottom of a concrete stairwell a short distance away that led up to the second level.

"Listen, Frederick," I began in an earnest attempt to appeal to his sense of leadership and responsibility. "I don't have to tell you that your grandmother is a very sick woman. She's battling a severe case of cancer and on top of that, she's trying to look after you and your siblings.

"And there's seven of you, top begin with. I'm talking seven very active, energetic, and spirited children. Are you following me?" I asked, peering over at him.

"I think so," he said as he jerked his head to the left as a squirrel appeared out of nowhere and dashed up a nearby tree.

"What I am saying is that your grandmother, and your brothers and sisters, are going to need your guidance and assistance. I know it's quite a burden to be placing on you but I'm sure your brothers and sisters look up to you, especially the younger ones, and your grandmother would certainly appreciate your help."

"I try to help out around the house and look out for my brothers and sisters but I want to have a life too and do things with my friends," he said, pulling out a comb and running it through his bushy hair several few times before putting it away.

"I understand all of that Frederick," I said. "But your grandmother would probably like to have a life of her own too but you know what? She's too busy looking out and caring for her grandchildren. I'm talking grandchildren she loves very much."

"Yeah, I see what you mean," he murmured. "But I am so tired of living in cramped spaces and being around my family all of the time. And the rules. Sometimes she treats me like I a little child. I want some time for myself, once in a while. God, I really wished I could go and live with my uncle."

"Where does your uncle live?" I asked.

"In Port St Lucie, Florida," he answered.

"Well, perhaps the day will come when you can arrange that. Just the same, I will talk to your grandmother about that possibility."

"That would be great," he said with a trace of a smile. "Don't get me wrong, I love my family and all but I just feel like I need more space than what I have here."

"I'm sure you do, and some of the others may feel the same way too," I added. "But while you're here, you might think about being more of an example for your younger siblings. I mean going to school and doing well in school.

"I'm telling you, you're not going to get too far in this world without a good education, Freddy."

"Yeah, I know. Everyone says that."

"Then seriously think about the friends you choose to be around," I said, making reference to the shady characters he had been seen associating with. "You don't want to follow behind the wrong crowd and end up in jail."

Frederick nodded his head, but said nothing, his gaze thoughtful.

"Come on, I'm through preaching," I said motioning for him to stand up. "Your grandmother probably does a better job of that than me."

He let out a slight chuckle as he stood up.

After I got grandma to sign off on my home visit, I left and headed south to SR-206 and on to Interlachen, Florida. Although I had my concerns about the older children and their adolescent issues and concerns, I finally felt good about their housing situation. If any family needed help it was this family.

The following day I called the father of six of the seven Browning children, who was currently holed up in a jail in East Palatka. I wanted to visit with him but the Department of Corrections presented me far too many hoops to jump through to visit in person so I arranged to have a phone conference with him at a predetermined time instead. When we finally talked, I apprised him of his family's improved situation and asked him if he was going to be more involved in his children's life after he got out of jail. He assured me that he was going to find a job, find a place for them to live, and be the father he had failed to be in the past. He told me that he would be getting out in four months. I knew that he and the children's mother were no longer in a relationship so I didn't bring her up, except to say that she had indicated that she wanted to complete her case plan and gain custody of the children after she was released from jail. He made no comment on that revelation.

Later that day I talked to the mother of the Browning children and she practically said the same thing Mr. Browning had said, about being more involved with the children and getting a job and finding a place to stay. Time would tell if they were really serious about this or were just handing me a line. I emphasized to the mother, as I had with the father, that the children's grandmother was very ill and that they had better start thinking about what was in the best interest of their children once they were released. I did not know if either parent knew it but Mrs. Browning had told me that she was terminally ill. She wasn't expected to live through the year. As for the parents being made aware of this, I would leave that up to the family members to tell them.

That evening I completed four home visits and afterwards, headed for my own home. I arrived at my castle deep in the woods around 8:00 PM, tired and hungry. In my hand was a bag containing a couple of Taco Bell menu items. It was a good thing I lived alone, especially with refried beans on the menu.

The fog hovering around was thick early the following morning as I made my way along SR-207 towards St Augustine. Because of the distances, I often left my house in the dark. Once I got to SR-206, I made a right turn and headed east. A mile down this stretch a couple of tall and weird looking birds trotted across the road in the fog. It was too late for me to do anything as I clipped one of them with my left front bumper. I continued on wondering why they just didn't fly across the roadway.

Around 9:00 AM we were all ushered into our cramped conference room to meet our new program manager. Her name was Karen Zeltzman, a former DCF employee, with a background in Child Protective Investigations and as a DCF training instructor. I didn't know her personally but I had met her once when I had to take a test required for the job and she was one of the instructors giving the test. Karen stood around 5'5" and had short dark hair that was cut pixie-styled. She had brown piercing eyes. It was apparent that she was from the northeast part of the country but her heritage was Hebrew.

After the introduction and a short training session, the caseworkers returned to our area and gathered around in pockets to discuss the meeting we had just returned from and the new program manager. Of the five or so people who put in to become the assistant program manager, Myra, Elizabeth, and Allyson were the ones I could remember on the top of my head, Allyson had been selected to be the second in command just under Karen. She had recently returned from maternity leave. A few caseworkers thought she had not worked as a caseworker long enough to be considered for the job. But she was, nevertheless. She was one of the few caseworkers with a juvenile justice background.

Not one for getting caught up in office gossip; I returned to my desk to review two new cases I had just received. I had an ESI staffing (early services intervention) scheduled for that afternoon on the two cases and I wanted to get up to speed on them. The first case was the Isaiah Hanson case. Isaiah was a two year old child who tested positive for marijuana at birth. The parents were offered services at the time, including Healthy Start and parenting classes. A year later, a second report came in alleging inadequate supervision. It appeared that the father, Aaron Hanson, was cleaning a pistol in the living room and was attempting to empty the chamber of the gun when the firearm went off. The bullet struck the child's mother, Roxanne Henri, in the leg. The child was in the room at the time of the incident. When the police and rescue arrived, they observed a bong used for smoking marijuana in the dining room. Both parents admitted to using marijuana that day and when tested, both parents tested positive for marijuana. Closing the case file, I grabbed the next one and opened it.

The second case was the James Peterson case. While taking James to Florida, mom picked up her paramour from prison along the way. He had been imprisoned for auto theft. The mother, her paramour, and the child took four days to make the drive to Florida. Along the way the three shared the same motel room when they stopped over for a couple of nights throughout the trip. During those overnight stays, the child was alleged to have been exposed to sexual intercourse between his mother and her paramour. The child, James, was said to be in fear of his mother's paramour. Approximately six months earlier the paramour was alleged to have sodomized the child.

Moving on I gazed over the child's statement which read: the child was interviewed by CPT (child protective team) and disclosed that when he was about eight or ten years old, there was an occasion when he awakened to find Mr. Copeland naked behind him. The child said "Leonard Copeland touched my behind with his dick." The child also stated that Mr. Copeland had placed his mouth on his privates many times in the past and that he could not move because Mr. Copeland was on top of him. The child informed his mother of this but said she did not believe him and refused to report it.

Next, I read over the mother's statement: the mother, Marianne Blakely, was not completely convinced her child was telling the truth. She stated that she believed her son was lying because he had never been left alone with the paramour. She believed that both grandparents were putting the child up to this. She believed her son was being coached because her mother and mother-in-law do not like Black people. Leonard, her paramour, was Black. Asked by the CPI if she would terminate her relationship with Mr. Copeland, because of the child's allegations, mom said, "Place my son with my mother-in-law because I want to be with Leonard."

The case file record went on to say that the biological father of the child, Mr. James Peterson Sr. was non-offending, but not actively involved with his son and has not expressed an interest in getting custody of his son. He made it quite clear that he was unable to care for the child but would support the child financially once he was placed with the paternal grandparents. To date, the grandparents reported having received no financial assistance from the child's father. The biological father has a history of physically abusing the boy.

It was also noted that the boy was placed with his paternal grandparents, Fredrick and Harriett Peterson. As for mom, she moved to Jacksonville where she and Leonard lived in a singlewide trailer. Though mom was granted supervised visitation, she and the paternal grandparents did not get along. With that, I closed the case file and leaned back into my chair. Exhaling, I pondered how affected this boy was emotionally and how stable he was mentally, that is, if his allegations were true. Just being in the same room while his mother was being ravished by a man he despised and feared was enough to affect him psychologically and for the remainder of his life. I'm sure to her family's' chagrined, mom was known to have traded sexual favors to raise funds to buy the drugs she used. Who would doubt for a minute this was not the best situation for any child to be raised in? I thought. And his father was no help to him. He had gone off and had other children with his current girlfriend and seemed to have written James, his oldest son, off. And from what I had read, he had been accused of physically abusing the boy when he was involved in his life for a brief spell.

Closing the file, I shut my eyes momentarily and thanked the Almighty that I did not have as bad a rearing as this boy had. Sure, I had it rough but nothing that ever came close to this.

Clearing my desk of files and important paperwork, I headed out for an early lunch. I returned to finish up a few documents I needed for the ESI staffing that afternoon. By 1:00 PM, I was ready to drive over to the Lightner Building where the Child Protective Investigators' and the attorneys for the state offices were located in the historic district of St Augustine.

I arrived at the Lightner Building an hour later and parked across the street from what was once a top-notch hotel called the Alcazar Hotel. The hotel was built by railroad tycoon Henry Flagler. Flagler was once a partner in the oil business with the world's first billionaire, John D. Rockefeller. Built in the late 1880s, the hotel hosted major events including national swimming championships before it was purchased and turned into a museum and parts of it government offices. The most scenic aspect of the building that drew me to it was the courtyard which had a breathtaking display of tropical trees and plants and a huge picturesque pond full of large tropical fish with a walkover bridge at its center. Weddings were held in the courtyard on a weekly basis.

As I often referred to it in jest, the usual suspects were present at the staffing, which included my supervisor Tyrone, two Guardian ad Litem personnel, the Child Protective Investigator, his or her supervisor, and the attorney for the state. What occurred at these staffings was that the investigator would discuss the circumstances on why a child was removed and sheltered by them. Insight would be provided on the conditions at the home or site at the time the child was taken into protective custody. In short, the investigator shared what was observed, why it was felt the child or children were at risk, and where the children were placed. If mom went to a shelter for abused women, her whereabouts would be discussed. If a parent was arrested and incarcerated, that would be discussed. Questions would be asked and services discussed and if the paperwork was in ordered, the case would be turned over to us, Child Protective Services, or, as they are known in Florida since being privatized, Community Based Care.

After both of my cases were staffed, I returned to the office to go online and get directions from MapQuest for my new cases. I decided to visit Aaron Hanson and Roxanne Henri of the Isaiah Hanson case. This is the case where the mother of the child was accidently shot in the leg by the child's father. The couple resided on Anastasia Island.

Grabbing my clipboard and notepad and my MapQuest printout, I headed out. Turning right on CR 312, I drove east until I crossed a bridge over the Intercostal waterway and onto Anastasia Island. Going down as far as I could east on CR 312, I made a right turn on A1A and headed south. Six miles later I arrived at the mobile home community where Isaiah lived. Because law enforcement viewed the discharging of the gun an accident the child was not removed from the home. Aaron was charged with reckless endangerment, though.

Aaron met me at the door of the singlewide mobile home and led me inside where I was introduced to Roxanne. The young couple and I sat down on the sofa that had a coffee table with a glass top positioned in front of us. The home was well furnished and comfortable. I did not notice any safety hazards. Both Aaron and Roxanne appeared to be affable individuals. Roxanne, twenty-two years of age, was wearing daisy dukes and looking the part of an attractive country girl. Aaron looked like he was only two or three years removed from high school, although he was actually twenty six years old.

For the next twelve minutes or so, he reconstructed what happened when Roxanne was accidentally shot. He even had her show me the bullet wound she had sustained that day in her leg. The kicker was that on the day she was shot, she told me that she was actually holding their son in her arms. I never read that in the case file.

After I went over what services they needed to get started on, case plan-wise, in order to close out their case, mom went to wake Isaiah up. She returned with the diapered two-year old in her arms a minute later. As I stood to greet him, he let out a yawn then clung even closer to his mother as he gazed in my direction.

Once Aaron signed my home visit form, I departed. I was convinced, much like law enforcement that the two were a genuine fit, a caring and loving couple, and that the shooting was unintentional. Aaron just happened to do a dumb thing one day like cleaning a gun without checking it and with it pointed in the direction of where his better half and his child were seated.

Heading south on AIA I made a right turn on SR-206 and drove west until I arrived at US1, turned left and headed south. My next stop was going to be the James Peterson residence, the boy who had been *allegedly* sexually abused by his mother's paramour.

Chapter 5

I pulled my Cadillac onto the property of James Peterson's grandparents twenty minutes later. The doublewide manufactured home was located in Flagler Estates. A winding handicap ramp led up to the main entrance. Off to the side of the house was a shed. Several cats sat on the ramp and its wood railing peering at me. There had to have been at least five of the felines lounging about.

James' paternal grandmother Harriett answered the door. I presented my ID and introduced myself. Harriett was in her early sixties and attired in a long dress the type worn by women of the Amish faith. Her hair was silvery gray and her eyes just as gray. Offering up a warm friendly smile, she ushered me inside. To my left sat her husband, Fredrick Peterson, a robust looking man in his mid-sixties. He looked like he might have been asleep in his chair before my arrival. He had salt and pepper hair and wore glasses, yet he had a rustic look about him. Harriett introduced the two of us and he gave me a warm greeting.

The aroma of kielbasa and sauerkraut hung in the air. I thought I detected the aroma of seasoned cabbage as well. The house was cleaned and well furnished, with a sofa and two chairs, one a leather padded chair with two parallel rolls of decorative antique brass nail heads lining the outer perimeter of it, and a coffee table. Sitting atop an adjacent table was a large dollhouse. The matriarch of the house built it, she told me after watching me walk over to it. I told her that I had always been fascinated with people who built model cars, planes and ships, as well as dollhouses and other miniature things.

"Here, take a seat, please," Harriett insisted after I turned my attention back to the business at hand. "I'll go and get James she said in a soft spoken voice. He's in his bedroom."

As I sat down, Fredrick told me that he built miniature railroad towns and landscapes with electric trains running through them. He promised to show them to me before I left.

Harriett reappeared in the corridor with James in tow. Though he was only thirteen, he was a good size boy. He had reddish hair and freckles. He was slightly pudgy but not plump. He was polite and greeted me enthusiastically.

"Glad to meet you James," I began. "I'm Mr. Carl Benjamin."

"Are you going to be my new caseworker?" he asked.

"Yes, I am," I replied reclaiming my seat.

James remained standing.

"When am I going to be able to visit with my mother?" he asked.

"Your grandparents and I are going to discuss that before I leave," I answered.

"Good," he said spiritedly. "I hope it's soon. Should I go back to my room while you guys discuss this?"

"Yeah, why don't you do that, James," Mr. Peterson said.

"Okay!" the youngster quipped and took off for his room.

In a hushed voice Harriett said, "We tried to do supervised visits with the mother here but it just didn't work out and she's not welcomed here anymore."

"What happened?" I asked.

Leaning forward, Fredrick broke in, saying, "She would drive down here with that Leonard guy and have him sit outside in the car and I didn't think that was right."

"Maureen just did not seem to care that this man abused this boy," Harriett chimed in. "And James is afraid of him. That's why we stopped the visits here."

"What about meeting her somewhere other than here with James?" I asked.

"We're at least 12 miles away from St Augustine and we just don't have the gas money to do that on a regular basis," Fredrick said.

"I'm sure she told you that we don't want her here because she's seeing a Black man," Harriett quietly said, as she rearranged a couple of magazines on the coffee table.

"Actually, I haven't talked to Maureen yet," I professed. "But I was aware that she had made claims that you all were prejudice."

"Prejudice, my god," Fredrick grumbled, his forehead wrinkled like the prunes one of my health conscious co-workers ate on a daily basis. "I'm not surprised she'd tell others that we're prejudice or racists or whatever you want to call it. Hell, that woman wouldn't know prejudice if it smacked her in the face a dozen times."

"Listen, I understand the sensitivities here," I began to explain. "I understand that you don't want the guy accused of molesting your grandson on your property and you have that right. As for mom, I believe she has her paramour drive her down here because she probably doesn't have the means to get here, or doesn't have a license to drive."

"I don't understand why that man is allowed to walk the streets after what he did to James," Harriett grimaced.

"They ought to shoot the sonavabitch, if you ask me," Fredrick snapped with a frown. "But he's allowed to go on with his life as if nothing's ever happened."

Still talking in a hushed voice, I said, "Look, as far as I know, the police are still investigating the matter. But I will check up on their progress from time to time. That, I can do."

"It probably won't do any good," Fredrick complained. "They'd rather spend their time going after people who have a cold beer in their own backyard after work than go after real hardcore criminals."

Wanting to move the conversation along, I went into solution mode. "Listen, this is what I'm going to do about these family visitations. The way their going now, James will never get to see his mother and the court order expressly states that mother and son are to have regular visits.

"Now, I've already looked into the file and saw that you and your wife are eligible for relative caregiver funds. I'm turning the paperwork in tomorrow. Once you start getting these funds that should cover the cost of gas to the visits.

"Now, there's a Dairy Queen restaurant just off of US1 and I-95. You know where it is, I'm sure."

"Yes, we know where it is," Harriett said.

"Good. I can have his mother meet me at my office and I can lead her there." Dairy Queen was the halfway point between the grandparents' house and my office. Mom would be commuting here from Jacksonville, some sixteen miles north of St Augustine. "You two can bring James to the restaurant. How's that?" I asked.

"I think that's fair enough," Fredrick said. "As long as we don't have to have anything to do with her."

"Fred's right," Harriett said. "I think that's fair for everyone."

"How soon will it be before we start receiving these funds?" Fred asked, as he straightened his glasses on his nose with his forefinger. Almost in the manner Phoebe was always repositioning her glasses.

"Next month, I believe," I said. "Can't you start bringing James to these visits before then?"

"I imagine we can," Fred answered. "I just could not do this on a long term basis without any additional funds. Like most people, we're on a fixed income."

"James' father, is he doing any better getting involved with his son?" I asked, leaning back and crossing my legs.

"Not really," Harriett said.

"My son has been here maybe twice and has never taken this boy anywhere and never spends quality time with him," Fred answered.

"Why is that?" I asked.

"His girlfriend doesn't want James around," Harriett explained before going off to check on her food cooking in the kitchen.

"I see," I murmured.

From a distance down the hall a voice cried out, "Can I come back out now?"

"He probably was listening the whole time," Fred whispered with a smile before crying out, "I guess you can come out now James."

James reappeared within a matter of seconds.

"When can I see my mom?" he asked.

"I hope to arrange something at the beginning of next week," I answered, peering up at the young lad. "But I have to talk to your mother first and see what her schedule is like."

"Okay," he said understandably. "Hey, did grandpa tell you about our train projects?"

"He mentioned that he built railroad towns for his train sets but I didn't know you were in on it too."

"Yes, grandpa's teaching me how to build towns and now I'm pretty good at it," James said with what had to be his trademark effervescent smile. "Would you like to see it?"

"Sure," I replied, standing up. "But if it is alright with your grandparents, I'd like for you to show me your room first."

"Sure, go ahead," Fred said.

James led me to his room while talking the entire time about his train project. Once inside of his bedroom, which was surprisingly clean and organized for a preteen boy, I let him tell me about some of the drawings and posters on his wall and then about

36

some of his computer and video games. I then asked him about school and I also asked him how he liked staying with his grandparents. I knew that as a young and energetic child it must have been a challenge for him, as well as his grandparents, to match each other's pace and energy level.

Overall, he loved his grandparents and didn't mind being where he was but he desperately wanted to be reunited with his mother. I fully understood that. As for school, he said he was making good grades and always kept up with his homework. After our chat, he led me back into the other room where we met grandpa. The two of them led me into another room with three tables of varying sizes. The large table was the foundation for an expansive town with houses, churches, stores, government buildings, and playgrounds. Of course, there were railroad tracks with railroad trains throughout the miniature community. Fred turned them on and let me watch as the trains made their way through the town and over rivers and through tunnels.

Another table supported one of his incomplete projects. And then there was the third table that had a community layout that James was working on. This was an incomplete project but obviously still a work in progress. Both grandpa and grandson gave me a quick schooling on the hobby of railroad trains and how the communities were made. Harriett offered me a drink. I accepted a cold bottle of water.

An hour after my arrival, which was about the amount of time I spent on an initial visit, I departed. I left knowing a lot more about the case and a lot more about model trains.

The following afternoon I got a surprise visit by Sergio Labriano, Sr. at the office. Though in his mid-twenties, he could have easily passed for a senior in high school. With an almond colored complexion, he looked like he had mixed blood in him. Black and Latin, I would venture to guess. His hair was bushy and unkempt.

When I came upon him he was talking with his former Independent Living counselor Rory. Sergio, I had discovered, came up through the foster care system himself. Rory was the one who had alerted me to Sergio's presence and was the one to introduce us. Sergio talked in a calm and pleasant voice and I could see by his good looks, he was a lady's man, a real charmer. But nearly all batterers were known to be charmers, I reminded myself. After Rory finished talking to him I sat down to talk to him alone.

"As you already know, I'm the caseworker on your son's case," I began leaning forward slightly in my chair. "That includes the child's mother Alyson and yourself. My question to you is this, are you interested in being involved with your son?"

"Definitely," he declared as he eyed me. "Yes, I want to be involved in my son's life."

"I am glad to hear that Sergio," I said, nodding my head. "But from what I've heard and from what I've read in the case file, you seem to spend a lot of time in jail."

"Yeah, I know," he murmured, then attempted to explain why. "I keep doing dumb things that violate my probation and I have to stop that."

"You got that part right," I replied.

"I know I need to get my act together. Honestly, I really want to be there for my son," he continued. "I also want to go to school and finish my GED and I want to get a decent job. I'll do whatever you want me to do to complete my case plan."

"Well, for starters, just like you said, you have to stay out of jail," I stressed. "You're not doing your son or yourself any favors being behind bars."

"And I'm tired of being incarcerated, believe me."

"Look, as far as seeing your son, you have to show up in court first," I told him. "That's a court order, not mine. Are you willing to do that?"

"Mr. Carl, I'm ready to do whatever it takes, I swear," he said, though I wasn't at all convinced. "You see, that's one of the reasons why I came here today, to try to get my life straightened out."

"Well, I hope you are right," I said as I fixed my eyes on his.

"Please, just tell me what I need to do, Mr. Carl," he pleaded.

"You can first show up for court in two days," I said. "We'll take it from there after you show up."

"I'll be there," he promised.

"Okay, see you then," I quipped we both stood up. Shaking hands, we parted company.

I wasn't back at my desk for five minutes before Schquana, our beloved clerical guru, approached me to let me know that I had a visitor in the main lobby. She said it was Alyson Jenson, Sergio Labriano, Jr.'s mother.

That's odd, I thought. Just minutes after seeing the child's father, the mother suddenly pops up out of nowhere. And the two are not supposed to be involved, at that, according to what I had been told.

"Thanks Schquana," I said as I stood up to go and meet with the mother for the first time.

Exiting our secured area, I walked down a short narrow corridor which led into the main lobby. It was just enough of a walk to prepare oneself mentally for the unexpected.

I found Alyson sitting on a lobby chair. With three other Black women sitting around her, I managed to ID her right off the bat. Perhaps I saw a little of her son in her features, I just don't know. She was slightly petite but proportionally built. And she dressed well. I could see her working in the nursing field. What I really wanted to know was whether or not both parents had come to the office together. If they had arrived together, it wasn't a good sign from the mother. The message I would garnish from such collusion was that mom was not sincere about regaining custody of her child. The thought was disconcerting. I loathed people who placed drugs and their romantic relationships before their children.

After introducing myself, I escorted her back into our wing of the building and found a vacant room where we could talk without distraction.

"So, how are you and how may I help you Ms. Jenson?" I started off.

"My mother told me that you stopped by a few days ago and wanted to speak with me," she answered. Alyson did not say much when we headed back into my work space. Just shy of being labeled petite, she was an unassuming young woman who did not smile much and seemed a tab uncomfortable. I was interested in why.

"Ms. Jenson, may I call you Alyson," I asked.

"Please do," she said, looking a little more relaxed.

"Thank you. You can call me Carl."

"That's fine too," she said with a nervous smile.

"Actually, I just wanted to meet with you before we headed into court two days from now. I wanted to get your take on whether or not you plan on getting your own place and have your son returned to you."

"That's what I am working on now," she said. "I've already started my parenting classes and domestic violence classes. I have stable employment and I am working on finding me an apartment."

"You're doing a lot more than the father of your child is doing, that I can say," I quipped. "And speaking of your child's father, I just had a brief meeting with him. I'm just curious. Did you two come here together?"

"No, we did not come here together," she declared. "He knew that I was coming here and he followed me in his friend's car. I'm not thinking about Sergio."

"Well, I hope you are right Alyson," I came back. "It wouldn't look good in court that you are still involved with your son's father, that is, if you hope to have your son returned to you."

"And I do, I swear to God!" She said and quite adamantly.

"Okaay," I murmured. "We'll leave it at that."

"I just want my son back, that's all."

"Just keep on working on your case plan and it'll happen," I assured her. "By the way, where are you working at?"

"Arby's Restaurant," she answered.

"Well, I have nothing else to cover," I said, collecting my notepad and clipboard. "Do you have any questions?"

"What time is court?"

"Court starts around 9:30 in the morning two days from now."

"I'll be there."

"See you then," I said as I shook her hand and escorted her out to the main lobby. I hovered near a window in the narrow corridor to see if she and Sergio hooked up before she reached her car. I did not see any signs of him. For her sake, I hoped she was telling me the truth about not coming here with him.

Chapter 6

Two months had gone by since the court date with Alyson Jenson and Sergio Labriano Sr., who never made it to court that day. It seemed as though he had violated his probation, yes again, and just one day after we had talked, and was therefore jailed. Some people just never learn. Since that time I was assigned a number of what I considered weird cases. Two made the local newspaper. One case involved a mother and her teenaged daughter. Both decided one evening to go to the home of the young girl's ex-boyfriend with the intent to burn down his trailer. They had brought along a container of gasoline to ensure that the job got done. Both mother and daughter were arrested before they could fully carry out their scheme of arson. Because the daughter was a minor, we got involved. The second high profiled case involved a mother who decided to get drunk one evening and play poker with her son and his teenaged male friends. Disgusted, her son left the room. At the time, the mother was estranged from her husband, who worked on the police force in St Augustine. Then finally, there was the case of a mother and child, who were found by law enforcement on the side of Interstate 95 wrapped in a blanket and mom praying. The mother stated that she had run out of gas while traveling from Palm Bay, Florida to Oklahoma and had pulled off the road, nearly driving into a pond. Mother was observed to be speaking in tongues and waiting for the leader of the Smashing Pumpkins rock band to come and save her and her son. Mother was Baker Acted and the son, Eli was placed into protective custody by the Department. It was determined later that mom had gotten hold of some bad marijuana, perhaps laced with something else. These cases, though sad and deplorable made for an interesting read.

Things at the office seemed to go smoothly, especially with the latest personnel changes and transitions that had occurred at the upper echelon level. A few more top level people had resigned and moved on. For the most part, I was too busy to keep up with the changes or understand their ramifications. I just knew that things were much different than they were when Mrs. Joanne Johnston presided over us.

Karen, the new program manager, and I appeared to get along well. We had a mutual respect for one another, it appeared. But it was apparent to me, and a few others, that office cliques were taking form. There seemed to be two camps; the group that hovered around Karen and the group that seemed to want no part of any job related, close knit, social club, of sorts. A loner for most of my life and working career, I didn't associate in that way, not even during my navy days. Yes, I did the group luncheons, birthday and maternity parties, and Thanksgiving and Christmas gatherings, but it was always job related and inclusive of all caseworkers and staff members. Overall, I went to work to do a job, not socialize. But if I made a friend or two along the way, much like Phoebe, then so much the better.

$\mathcal{A}$fter listening to my voice mail messages, I prepared myself to conduct a supervised visit with the Jameson/Steel family at a popular playground on Anastasia Island just off the beach. I had the case for nearly two months but the mother, named Alisha Jameson, had made little progress with her case plan during that time. She was attending parenting classes and substance abuse classes but had dropped out. Once her visitation rights had been taken away by the court, she decided to resume working on what she needed to do to have her children returned to her and her visitation rights were restored. Only one of the children's fathers appeared interested in working on a case plan. The oldest child, and only boy, John Steele, who was now eleven, had been brought to a local hospital with a swollen tailbone after allegedly being lifted and thrown down on a hardwood floor by his stepfather, Jeremy Jameson, who was the father of John's three younger sisters and his mother's husband. There were conflicting stories from the child's stepfather and the child and the mother, who seemed to agree with her husband's account. Mr. Jameson claimed he and the boy were horsing around when John was tossed by him and was injured. John said that he was lifted and thrown down. For the child's protection, he and his sisters were removed and placed in foster care since there were no family members that could take the four children in.

There was John Steele, a quiet but bright young boy who was interested in science and nature and, most of all, collecting bugs and insects. He also loved dragon-lore. Overall, he had a good rapport with his parents, although he could be mildly defiant at times. The blonde haired, blue-eyed identical twins, Sherrie and Shelly, were outgoing and energetic. At times, they could be just as defiant and difficult to manage as their older brother. Like John, the twins were in counseling. Shannon, the youngest at four, was cute as a button and adorable as they come. She had blonde hair as well as her sisters and the cutest dimples unrivaled by other girls her age. However, this little five year old tyke could be quite a handful, at times. Fortunately, most of her energy was expressed through the normal channels of child expression: talking, playing, running, drawing, and watching television. I am uncertain how much she was aware of it but today was her birthday, June 5th.

Going outside, with a child's car seat in hand, I placed it in the rear of the car, entered on the driver's side, and my cranked my engine up. It was an inferno inside, thanks to the 88^0 weather. After lowering all of the windows, I turned the air-conditioning on, put on my sunglasses, and headed over to Brandt's Daycare at 142 Masters Drive in St. Augustine where I would pick little Shannon up and drive her to her birthday bash on Anastasia Island. In the beginning the family and I used to meet at a popular playground between US1 and San Marco adjacent to the main library. There was a well-known and very popular carousel on the grounds as well.

After a month of meeting there, I changed our meeting location to the Anastasia Island playground because of the heavy traffic and parking difficulties at the old location. Besides, being a navy veteran, I loved the salty air and the panoramic view I got when I looked out over the ocean. I also loved to hear the ocean waves crashing against boulder sized rocks and I loved to watch flocks of pelicans and seagulls soar to and fro up above.

During the visits, John would be dropped off by his foster care parent and the twins would be brought to the visit by their foster care mother, a woman named Marge Hamilton. She was new to the foster care business. Unlike John's foster care father, Paul, who would leave then come back later to pick him up, Marge always stayed for the duration of the visits. She and the children's grandmother were around the same age and the two loved to talk, even over the phone. Alisha, the children's mother, seemed to behave with indifference with Marge, and quite understandably since this was the woman who was caring for one half of her brood. Jealousy, perhaps, was what I wrote it off as being and nothing more. But usually, after a few minutes had passed, mom would warm up to her daughters' surrogate mother. Only when Marge would bark out a command or give the girls some instructions would mother's eyes turn piercing and somewhat menacing.

There was an earlier incident which had occurred during a family visitation where Marge grabbed Sherrie by the arm, as she sprinted by where we were sitting, shook her, and told her to stop running. I looked at Marge, mother looked at me, and grandma looked at all three of us. Right then I knew Marge and I needed to have a talk in private and soon. But first, I wanted to calm mom down. She had a look that could kill. I asked grandma and Marge to take the children outside. I told them that I just needed to go over a few things about mom's case plan and didn't need the children around. Besides, the owner of the snack bar had already warned us about the children running inside the space. Just the same, I sensed that grandma knew why I ushered her, the children, and Marge off. And she was right, to calm her daughter down. When the coast was clear, mom spoke up.

"Did you see the way that woman grabbed my daughter and shook her?" Alisha blurted out with eyes of brimstone and fire. "Who does she think she is?"

"Yes, I saw it and I am going to have a talk with her," I assured her.

"I mean, is this the kind of protection the state claims it provides for children they remove from their parents?" she ranted, and justifiably.

"Listen Alisha," I injected with a firm voice. "I am just as put off as you are but you're going to have to let me handle this, and I will as soon as we're through talking. "Alright, but if that woman puts her hands on my daughter again, it's going to be WWIII up in here."

"Look, I'm not going to let that happen," I said, again in a firm voice and with a look that conveyed the message 'don't tread on me'."

"Alright," she said in apparent surrender.

"Please, on your way out don't say anything to Marge," I asked. "I'm going to get her now."

"You don't have to go," she said, rising up. "I'll tell her that you want her when I go out."

I eyed her for a second but did not utter a word.

"Look, I promise I'll be civil, okay," she said.

"Okay," I replied, as I leaned back in my chair with my eyes still trained on her.

Marge appeared inside of the snack bar a minute later. I could tell by her smiling face she had no clue why she had been summoned by me.

"Please have a seat," I said, leaning forward, my arms resting on the tabletop, my hands clasped.

"What's up?" she said after sitting down.

"Marge, don't take this the wrong way but you cannot snatch and jerk these children around like you just did with Sherrie," I said, my voice strained.

"God, I didn't think that I did anything wrong other than to stop her from running about. I mean, the owner was already warning us about them dashing about the area."

"Marge, you were pretty rough with Sherrie. Look, I know you are new to the foster care business but these visits are supposed to be between the family members and the children. If the children act up, it is their mother's place to correct them, not yours," I emphasized. "I mean, I cannot get a clear picture of how mom interacts with her children if you will not give her a chance to interact with them."

"Well, I really don't see what the fuss is all about, I really don't," she continued as she blinked her eyes.

"Marge, I need you to see what all of this fuss is about because if I cannot get you to see it, I will have to make a determination whether or not you will be allowed to stay during these visits.

"Furthermore, if I am a witness to you grabbing one of those children like that again, I am going to have to consider removing them from your care. Believe me, that will not look good for your chances of having other children placed with you," I warned.

"What I did was that serious?"

"Yes, it was."

That was then and this was now. To her credit, I had not seen Marge behave that way again, at least, not in public and not around me or the twins' family members.

When I arrived at the daycare center, a group of young children were in the playground area either on swings, sliding down a couple of sliding boards, or running about playing chase.

Exiting my car I headed for the gated entrance, all the while scanning the playground area for Shannon. It wasn't long before I spotted her, and she me. As always, when she spied me, her eyes widened, along with her warm precious smile. Then she'd rush towards me until she was in my arms and I had lifted her up off of the ground and into my gentle embrace.

I checked her out for the remainder of the day, escorted her to my car holding her hand, secured her in the car seat in the rear of the Cadillac, and then we drove off. The ride to the island took about twenty minutes, thanks to traffic on US1. Once I made a left turn onto CR 312, traffic wasn't as bad.

We arrived at the playground just as her mother Alisha and grandmother Lorraine, and grandmother's friend, Frank, were pulling up in their station wagon. We all converged on a table in a covered area of a combination bait and tackle shop and snack bar, which was adjacent to a dedicated pedestrian fishing pier that extended out into the Atlantic Ocean a good distance. The playground was just outside of the shop and snack bar facing the sandy beach.

While mom set the table with paper plates, Frank returned to the station wagon to retrieve little Shannon's birthday cake. Alisha returned to the car to get a bag of chips and pretzels and a bucket of Kentucky Fried Chicken. Containers of Cole slaw and baked beans were the side orders placed on the wood table. It wasn't long before John was dropped off by his foster care parent, Paul, and Marge pulled up in her SUV with the twins.

For the next hour the children ran about, ate, ran about some more, played and got wet in the sprinklers in one area of the playground. Midway through the visit we all gathered around the table and sang happy birthday to Shannon. After cake and ice cream, we began to clean up the area. By now, John's foster care father had returned to pick him up. He had some cake and ice cream before they parted. Marge and the twins were next to take off. I allowed Shannon, our little birthday girl, an extra few minutes with her mother and grandmother, then we took off. I returned her to her foster care home off of SR 16 a mile south of I-95. Then I headed for home.

Chapter 7

The following week I spent two days in Tampa Bay, Florida with a few of my co-workers, including Phoebe for a conference. Karen was there as well as our assistant program manager Allyson Mackenzie and her husband Mike, who had recently been promoted to supervisor. There was a lot of talk about nepotism involving those two, for certain. And sure, I kept my eyes and ears opened but I just did not get myself caught up in these office issues like others did. But while there, that close knit group hung out together and Phoebe and I hung out together, along with a fairly new worker named Melody, who once worked in this same capacity in Collier County. When I headed a grant program at the health department in Putnam County, I included all of my staff when it came to hanging out, except on a few occasions when I needed to discuss something with one of them on a one to one basis. But I never allowed my staff to splinter off into cliques. At my agency, that appeared to be what was happening. You were either in the clique or outside of it, socially speaking, which was fine with me. The problem was that the clique rarely distinguished between what was after work social bonding and what was work related bonding. The same clique functioned socially both during work and after work. In time dissension grew amongst some of the caseworkers and staff members who were not in the clique, many who wanted no part of it to begin with. The problems I often heard discussed centered on the more notable conferences and training opportunities that presented themselves. It seemed as though certain people in the clique always seemed to get a foot up on everyone else and on a yearly basis. Only once in a while they'd add a new face to travel with them but the core members of the clique made certain that they went and first class. Aside from the conference in Tampa, I attended another two day event down in Daytona Beach, by myself. That was a lot of fun, you can imagine. I actually felt like I had been exiled for two days.

The day after my return from my conference I headed over to the Browning residence that afternoon. I had received a call from the apartment complex manager who wanted to talk to me in person. This was not a good sign. I called Mrs. Browning to see what she could tell me but she was not in. She had probably gone for her cancer treatment.

I arrived at the main office and met with Mrs. Townsend, the manager, in her office.

"I thought I'd call you since I know you are the caseworker and might have some influence on those children," she began, as her eyes met mine. She was in her mid-thirties, a brunette, and educated looking. She was wearing a form fitting black skirt and a fashionable white blouse. She was probably the high school homecoming queen and had probably majored in business administration in college. She appeared to be a capable woman but right now she seemed to be in dire need of my assistance.

"What's the problem?" I asked, returning my gaze to her, after looking at a family picture of her and her husband and their two children on top of her desk.

"It's the boys," she said with an urgency I had not heard from her before. "They have been banned from the computer lab and swimming pool because they're always acting up and talking out loud and leaving the area a mess. Now, I know that their grandmother is very ill and doing the best that she can with those children but someone needs to talk with those boys and see if they can talk some sense into their heads. We don't want to but we will evict the family if this behavior continues."

"I'll have a talk with them, Mrs. Townsend," I said. "But if I am able to get them to behave, will you allow them access to the computer room and swimming pool again."

"We certainly will, Mr. Benjamin," she assured me.

"Okay, I'll go and see if they're home."

"Thank you so much for coming out today," she said, rising up from her chair.

"It's part of my job," I declared soberly.

The stressed out manager led me out of her office and through the lobby and out the front door.

Outside, I took the concrete walkway that led to the family's complex. I arrived a few minutes later and rang the doorbell. Mrs. Browning greeted me at the door but this time with a worried look. Taking off my shoes, I followed her into the dining room where we sat down to talk.

"I just returned from my cancer treatment and just got your message on the phone," she began. "The office has been complaining about the boys and their behavior at the pool and computer lab."

"I know," I professed. "I just came from the main office. Mrs. Townsend asked me to come over so that she could talk to me. She told me that the boys had practically been banned from the main office area and swimming pool."

"That's correct, but I can tell you, my grandsons, though loud and sometimes hardheaded, are not responsible for all of the things that woman is saying they are responsible for," she assured me, as she wiped her forehead with a cloth. It was hot outside and she had been sweating, she told me, before returning home.

"Well, I'd like to talk to them and hear their side of the story when they return home," I added.

Looking at the wall clock, Mrs. Browning said, "They should be walking in the door any minute now. Could I get you something to drink?"

"Naah, thanks but I'm fine," I replied with a soft smile.

As if on cue, the doorbell rung and Mrs. Browning went to answer it. The youngest girl, Francine and her brother Françoise, one eight and the other nine years old, walked in with backpacks glued to their backs. They paused long enough to remove their shoes then entered the area where I was sitting and greeted me. Next Frances and Franklin, both boys around the ages of twelve and fourteen, entered next. Fanisha and Franco, one fifteen and the other sixteen, arrived next. The oldest boy, Frederick, called Freddy, who was eighteen, had gone down to Port St Lucie, Florida to live with his favorite uncle, having dropped out of school a month earlier.

After the children had gotten drinks and settled down, I had them all assemble in the living room area. I had the boys tell me their side of the story and what I got from them was that management seemed to blame them for everything that went wrong at the complex. They said that they had been suspected of breaking into an apartment and stealing some things. The boys denied doing this, though they said they had an idea who had broken into the apartment. As for the computer lab and swimming pool, they said they were having just as much fun as the other children there and behaved no worse than the other children but seemed to get blamed whenever management arrived on the scene.

"Perhaps it's because we're Black," Franco railed aloud.

"Perhaps," I answered. "Or perhaps it's because all of the kids there, including you boys, are just too loud and rumbustious."

After I heard from each child, I told them that I needed them to continue to have fun and enjoy themselves but to keep it all on the down-low, meaning, not raising unnecessary attention to themselves. I told them that if they did not tone it down, regardless of what other children were doing, they might be asked to leave the complex.

When I had finished with my pep talk with the children, grandmother and I talked a little while longer. She appeared tired and weak and her hair looked much grayer. In a short while, after some encouraging words I shared with her, I took off.

A year and half had passed by since I came to work for the Family Integrity Program and now Phoebe was talking about leaving the agency to go up north to spend more time with her mother and especially, her grandmother, who was not in the best of health. That saddened me, no doubt. Tired of the long hours and the stress of working in child protective services she had started up her own office and vacation home cleaning service with her daughter. I even helped her out one weekend. How she and her daughter did this on a regular basis confounded me. I was sore and thoroughly exhausted only after working one day with her. I must have cleaned out four condos during that day but because of my bad knee, something I had injured during my time in the navy, going up and down the stairs carrying bundles of dirty linen and fresh linen, buckets and mops, and cleaning agents, this activity wore me out. Anyway, I was happy to have been available to help my friend out. By now she had married a guy she had met in St Augustine and the two were in agreement that it was time to leave and head north. Within two months, Phoebe was gone.

A week after my friend and co-worker's departure I was assigned one of my most challenging cases to date, the Dennis Bowls Jr. case. Leaning back in my desk chair, I read through the file. It appeared that the maternal grandmother and legal custodian in the case, Darlene Sawgrass, tested positive for cocaine on a random drug screening by her probation officer. The sample was further tested by an independent lab because grandmother denied using cocaine. The sample came back positive for cocaine from the lab.

Grandmother had been on felony probation for unlawfully possessing a controlled substance without a prescription and the reckless operation of a motor vehicle. Sometime after that, the grandmother was requested to take a random drug screening for the Department but failed to supply enough of a sample to be tested.

Complicating things, the grandmother had been awarded temporary legal custody of the child listed in the case, through family court proceedings. This custody was based on the mother's instability and the father's incarceration (at the time). The grandmother's home was observed to be filthy and hazardous to the child's health and well-being.

Needing to explore a new placement for the child, the CPI made contact with the child's mother, Amber Sawgrass. It was determined that the mother's situation was still too unstable for her son to be returned to her. She was residing in a motel and was still unemployed and was lacking reliable transportation. In addition to this, the mother had been recently released from jail and was expecting another child, her third.

The main reason why the case came to our attention was that the child's unmarried parents were reported to be fighting all of the time, throwing objects and screaming at one another. Police were reported to have made several past calls to this couple's residence to quell other domestic violence issues with the couple. The report also stated that the mother was in the habit of leaving the child home alone while she took off to go shopping or do laundry. The child was reported to have had an infected belly button and his penis, not being circumcised, was not kept properly cleaned. Yes, I got to know almost every detail of every client's private life as a caseworker, no matter how raw the descriptions got. That was the nature of the business I was in.

As for the child's father's take on things, he admits to having had little contact with his son in the past because he was incarcerated for several years and because the mother usually blocked him from seeing his son. He admitted to getting in trouble with the law but stated that he paid the price for it and served his time. He also admitted having an alcohol problem in the past but has stayed away from it now. He received treatment for his alcoholism in prison and felt he was a better person because of it. He felt that the chance at rearing his son seemed challenging because the child was known to exhibit aggressive behavior, especially in daycare settings. But when the child was around him he noted that the child acted fine. He stated that the mother was out to make him appear like an unfit parent but it wasn't true. He stated that the mother, when she had custody of the child, was in the habit of exposing him to unethical situations. Dad said that the child once told him that he and his mother used to pretend to go to drug parties and pretended to smoke *weed* and drink alcoholic beverages.

Finally, the report said that all reasonable efforts to prevent or eliminate the need for removal of the child had been made but continuation of the child in the maternal grandmother's custody would have been contrary to the welfare of the child. Since the child's mother's situation remained unstable and uncertain, the child was placed with his biological father, who happened to be employed and had stable housing.

Closing the case file, I took a deep breath. This was a lot to absorb. But my review was far from over. To my amazement, this same mother had another active case with us that pertained to her two youngest children. The contents explained it this way: *Both mother and father are incarcerated at this time in St Johns County Jail. Mother already has an open case on her oldest child, Dennis Bowls Jr., who is now in his father's care. Mother recently tested positive for cocaine after a drug screening administered by her probation officer. Mother stated to her previous worker that she accidentally cut herself on a razor blade that had been used to draw lines of cocaine and believed that's how the drug got into her system. She said that she was reaching into someone's pants pockets and did not know a razor was in the pocket.*

Mother's most recent incident involved her and her former paramour, Don Juan Elders. The two had a history of domestic violence. Don Juan told the CPI that he gave the children's mother (Amber) some money to go buy diapers and some other items but she never came back. He said that he eventually found out that she had gone riding around with a friend smoking pot. When she returned in the morning to the hotel room, he blocked her from entering. The way he explained it was that he did not want to risk the children being placed in foster care because of her actions. As the two got into a physical altercation, Amber allegedly grabbed his shirt and tore it. That's when he brandished a gun. He said that someone called law enforcement but Amber left before they arrived. Not long after this incident, Amber was arrested for VOP due to that positive drug screen. Don Juan, himself, was eventually arrested for VOP being a felon found with a firearm in his possession. It was then the two Elders children were placed in Child Protective Custody. Mother was said to be pregnant again.

Don Juan and Amber were known to have a volatile relationship. Although three year old Deidra had Don Juan Elders' last name, he was not her biological father. Only Deon, the newborn, was his child. The couple will probably not reunite after they are released from jail, according to Amber's mother. The two have had difficulties throughout their relationship and would probably continue to if they got back together. As for the children, Deon had a slight respiratory problem. Other than that, he was fine. Deidra appeared to be developmentally delayed socially and possibly intellectually. But more tests needed to be done on her. Both children have been placed in foster care.

Closing the file, I jotted a few things on a piece of paper, questions I wanted to ask all three parents. Amber was Caucasian, as well as her son Dennis Bowls Jr. and so was Dennis Bowls Sr., the child's father. Her other beau, Don Juan Elders, was Black and the children, Deidra and Deon, were mixed. To date, Amber had yet to provide a clue in the case file who Deidra's father might be.

*A*round four that afternoon I took off to meet Dennis Bowls Sr. and his son, Dennis Bowls Jr., both who lived in a single wide trailer south on US1, about four miles from my office. I didn't know it at the time but he was staying with his girlfriend. We talked for about fifteen minutes during which time I met junior. He seemed harmless enough. He was soft spoken, not very talkative, but there was something about his piercing eyes that belied something more sinister inside. I know it sounded like something from the *Omen* or the 60s *Children of the Damned* movies but that was the vibes I got from looking into this six year old eyes. He had sandy blonde hair and a slight smirk, more than a smile. It was disconcerting to say the least. Demon child or not, I was the caseworker on the case and I had a job to do.

I left the home thirty minutes after my arrival and made my way towards Palatka. I had a dinner date with Ms. Cynthia and I didn't want to be late. There was a pretty decent Italian restaurant named Nikos' just off of SR-20 and CR-19 we sometimes ate at. We decided to dine there. Later we returned to her place to talk and watch a movie. Before leaving, she asked me to troubleshoot a computer problem she had been having. When I finally returned to Interlachen I got a phone call from my former fiancée, Renée. I don't know how she did it, but whenever I spent time with Cynthia, I seemed to get a call from her. It was like she had a built in *'spending-time-with-another-woman'* radar detector built inside of her. She was up in Alaska visiting her son who was stationed in the Air Force there. We talked briefly. She said she just wanted to know what I was up to. Nothing at all, I assured her. Nothing at all.

Chapter 8

True to her word, Alyson Jenson, Sergio Labriano Jr.'s mother, completed her case plan and during court earlier that morning, was granted custody of her son Sergio. A maintain and strengthened case plan had already been submitted to the court. If all went well, her case would be closed out in a couple of months.

I had a special session to attend in the judge's chambers that afternoon on another case. An hour after that I decided to meet Amber Sawgrass, and visit with two other mothers in jail there from two other cases assigned to me.

After I went through security, I was escorted to a waiting room on the second floor of the jail. They brought Amber in first and left us to talk.

Amber was a fairly attractive young woman who was in her late twenties. She had a bubbly personality, an easygoing smile, a toothy one at that, and though she was dressed in prison garb it did not take a seagoing sailor to see that in civilian clothing and a little makeup, this young lady was a potential knockout. Weighing around a healthy 130 lbs., or slightly more, considering she was pregnant, she was buxom as well. It was sad to me that such an attractive woman had nothing better to do with her life than to get caught up in drugs, bad choices in men, and prostitution.

"So you're my new caseworker," she said beaming.

"Yes I am," I replied.

"God, you're cute," she said flirtatiously as I waited for her to inquire about her children. "Are you married? You look like you are."

"Thank you," I said. "But I'm not."

"That's a surprise," she said as she fixed her eyes on mine. You would have thought she was a kid looking at a large lollipop

"Is there anything you'd like to ask me about your case?" I asked.

"Oh yeah," she said, clearing her throat. "How are my children doing?"

"Fine," I answered. "Dennis is with his father and your other two are in foster care, as you already know."

She frowned when she said, "I don't know why they placed my son with his father. That man is an alcoholic and he's been in prison."

"He's done his time, Amber, and he says he's clean," I said. "His background was looked into and he was cleared to take custody of his son."

"Well, he may have them fooled but not me," she leered. "Hell, he doesn't even get along with my son."

"They seemed to be getting along quite well when I visited them," I replied.

"I want out of here so that I can get my children back."

"Well, my advice to you is to stay out of trouble while you're here and it will be over before you know it."

"I've got two more weeks and I'm home free," she chuckled.

"What are you going to do once you're out of here?" I asked.

"I'm gonna find me a job and get my children back, including Dennis."

"Well, you do that and while you're at it, work on your case plan," I said. "I hear that they have a parenting class here in jail."

"I'm attending that," she replied.

"Good, that's really good," I murmured.

"God, I hate these prison clothes," she said with another frown. "You should see me when I'm all decked out, especially in a nice tight form fitting dress. I'm tell'n you, you would not be sitting there all calm and nonchalant like, Mr. Carl."

I smiled and dipped my head but said nothing. I knew that prison had an impact on women just as it had on men cooped up for months without the active presence of the opposite sex. I ventured to believe that any man sitting here would have been subjected to her flirtatious manner. It was just plain human nature. At least that's what I wanted to believe.

"Listen, I have two other mothers I need to talk to," I said returning my gaze to her. "It was nice meeting you and I will stop by next week to check in on you."

"It was nice meeting you too, Mr. Carl," she said, her eyes sparkling like sapphire, her mouth parted in a smile. "Yeah, I heard that you had some other mothers here who are in your case load. We've been talking to each other."

"Good," I said, setting my pen down. "You take care of yourself in here, okay."

"I will," she said. With a surreptitious winking of her eye, she stood up.

I decided to ignore her flirtatious gesture. "So, what do you want? A boy or girl?" I asked instead.

"It doesn't matter," she quipped. "When it's born I'm giving it up for adoption."

I turned and looked up at her with a thoughtful gaze but I did not respond. Perhaps it was better that she gave the child up considering the job she had done so far with the three she already had.

I spent equal quality time talking to my other two parents incarcerated there, one after another. An hour later, I left the county jail and its suffocating and claustrophobic interior and headed out to do some home visits.

A week later, I visited Amber and Elyse and Donna at the county jail. Elyse was a woman with a strong personality and two lovely young daughters, one eight years old and the other two years old. Both girls were in the custody of a friend of the family named Patricia. Elyse's problem was drugs and a bad choice of men as well. Until she got her act together, if she ever did, she was another wasted life. But she seemed to be handling life in jail very well. It wasn't her first time there and neither was it for Amber and Donna. Out of the three parents, Donna was the one having the hardest time adjusting to life behind bars again. She was not strong like my other two mothers. A drug addict herself, she was not coping well at all. During most of our session, she was breaking down and crying. She missed her two toddlers and wanted to get out of jail and do the right thing. But as long as I had her case, five months, she had not completed one thing in her case plan. I had my doubts about her ability to stay the course once she was let out in another week.

After my visit, I returned to the office. Tyrone, my supervisor, had resigned, I was told. I was surprised to hear that. Before the day ended I caught up to him. He said that he was heading out to California for a while. He had family there. He gave no specifics for why he was leaving but we often talked about the cliques that had developed within the agency. The two of us were like-minded in that particular area. Neither one of us wanted anything to do with whatever inner office drama reared its head there. Unlike me, I imagined Tyrone decided he needed to put more distance between him and the clique, much more. Heather, the other supervisor that was there when I joined the team had been transferred to another program in the agency. That left two vacancies opened for supervisor. A fairly new guy named Russ was selected for one position. The other position was taken by a young tall blonde named Susan Blackmon.

Returning to my cubicle, I sat down and began work on an initial family assessment. Ten minutes into it, I received a call from Aaron Hanson, the young rebel who had accidentally shot his fiancée in the leg. He sounded frantic.

"What is it?" I asked.

"I just shot at someone," he said.

"You just shot at someone?" I replied incredulously.

"Yeah, one of my neighbors and I got into an argument about a dent on my car and later he showed back up at my place with some of his boys," Aaron said. "I just felt that I had to defend my family so I reached inside of the door and grabbed my shotgun and discharged it just to scare them off."

"What happened next?" I asked. "I mean, did you hit anyone?"

"No," he quipped. "But they scrambled...all of them."

"I'm sure they're going to call the cops or return with a bigger shotgun," I replied, jotting all of this down.

"I'm ready for them if they do but more than likely, they've already called the cops."

"Do you have a permit for the gun?" I asked.

"Yeah, I do," he shot back.

"Good. Where's Roxanne and Isaiah?"

"They're in the house," he said. "They're fine. I just wanted you to know what happened so you wouldn't have to hear it from somebody else. I don't want to lose custody of my son, Carl."

"Well, depending on how things turn out, it will be up to the court, Aaron," I said unequivocally.

"I kind of thought it would be something like that," he mumbled. "Look, I have to go but thanks. I'll let you know if anything else develops."

"Okay, Aaron."

After hanging up the phone, I contacted my immediate supervisor, Allison Mackenzie, who said that it was law enforcement's call now, that is, if they showed up at the house. I concurred.

Two days later, Penny Boatwright showed up at my office. She said she was in the area and just stopped by to see me. She said that she would be attending counseling on a weekly basis and would be checking in with me, from time to time. I thanked her for stopping by and escorted her to the main entrance of the lobby.

Next on my agenda was a new case that was really an old case that was being reopened. Sitting down, I grabbed the file and opened it. It was the Ronika Dobson case. The sixteen year old Black female had been in a long-term relative caregiver situation with her aunt Tasha Clarkson for nearly five years. Over time, the relationship between the two soured and the aunt no longer wanted custody of her niece. A motion was submitted to the court to reopen the case so that a home study could be completed on the child's paternal grandmother, Lynn Sue Dobson. A subsequent court order approved the placement and the child was placed in the care of her paternal grandmother. That afternoon I would ride over to the grandmother's house and meet with Ronika.

An hour after I had set the Dobson case aside and started work on an upcoming judicial review, I was summoned to my program manager's office. I put away the files on my desktop and headed down the corridor to her office. The door was closed. I rapped on it gently. A voice told me to come in. When I opened the door, Karen and another upper level staff member were present and a guy I had never seen before. He was seated, like the others in the room. He was slightly heavyset and well shaved. He was a plump version of Kojack, the detective in the 70s television show that went by the same name. Though he was in civilian attire, this man had a badge positioned at his belt line. I was asked to have a seat.

"This is Carl Benjamin," Karen said to the stranger.

"Carl, this is inspector Callahan," she said, addressing me. "Mr. Callahan has a few questions to ask you."

Okay, I'm thinking. This probably has something to do with Aaron discharging his gun the other night.

"Mr. Benjamin, do you know why I am here?" he asked.

In all honesty, I did not know so that's what I told him.

"A few years ago you were working out of the Daytona Beach office and a report came into my office saying that you had been falsifying a home visit document. Remember any of that?" he asked me.

"I most certainly do," I quipped, now that I was fully appraised as to why he was here. "I told them the reasons behind why I used the documents and why I did not visit the child at the home. You want me to explain it all again?"

"Sure, why not?" he quipped.

I then recounted the agreement that I had with one of the workers in the Daytona Beach office who was supposed to visit the child in my case whenever she went to visit hers since both of our children were in the same foster care home. I said that at that time, we did not enter the information in the computers in Bunnell because the system was down more than it was up and when it was up, it was unreliable. I said that we'd send all of our paperwork down there to Daytona to have entered into the system until they straightened out the problem in Bunnell. The confusion came about because I used the home visit forms for my family visitations as well so that I could show that I made the visit. It was to cover my rear end, I explained." You see, there wasn't a form for family visitations, at that time.

"Well, I've been investigating your case for nearly two years now," he said. "Were you aware that you were being investigated?"

"No, I had no clue," I replied. "They had a meeting with me, placed me on a corrective action plan, and that was the end of it. I never heard about that incident again," I said. "As for why I didn't seem eager to visit the home, aside from the fact that I thought that I had someone taking care of that, I wasn't comfortable around the foster parent of the child," I explained.

"How's that?" the investigator asked me.

"She was always asking me when I was coming over for a visit and whenever we were doing the family visits at McDonald's, which was on a weekly basis, she was always over dressing for the visits with the child and the parents. Females can get away with saying that they feel uncomfortable around men but hardly anyone would believe a man saying that he felt uncomfortable around a woman, so I didn't say anything. I just thought my co-worker down in Daytona was seeing my child."

"Like I said, I've been investigating this case for nearly two years and what you're saying jives with what I came across," he began. "I saw no other incidents where you did not visit the home and I did see that you did use the home visit form to verify that you had made various family visitations.

"Now, I have spoken to your leadership here and they tell me that you are one of their top workers and that they have never had any complaints about your work. I reviewed the cases you worked on in Daytona and concluded that everything was in order. It is evident to me that you are a thorough caseworker.

"Frankly, guy, I have no evidence that you falsified anything and as far as I am concern, the matter is closed. I'm leaving it up to your program manager to check your current files to see if everything is up to snuff. But like I said, they have had nothing but praise for your work. If you have no further questions, that's all. I'm through," he chuckled.

"No, I haven't anything to ask," I replied.

"Here, this is your copy," he said as he handed me a folder which I took in my hand.

"Thanks," I said, glossing over the paperwork.

"This is a record of what was alleged and what was investigated and what was concluded," the investigator said.

"Thanks, again," I said, turning my gaze away from the package over at the investigator.

"You can go back to work now," Karen said, tossing me a smile and wink. "You're not in trouble or anything."

"That's good to know," I said rising up.

With that matter out of the way, I returned to my cubicle, sat down, and exhaled a sigh of relief. I had no clue that for two years I was being investigated. Not a single clue.

That afternoon, I walked over to my Cadillac and fired up the engine and put the air-conditioner on full arctic blast until the car cooled down. Then I donned my sunglasses and drove over to Hastings, Florida to meet Ronika Dobson and her grandmother, Mrs. Lynn Sue Dobson. I arrived at County Line Road thirty minutes later and found the house, a singlewide, a quarter of a mile away on my right. I backed my car onto the property, through a narrow entrance way that crossed over a deep culvert, parked, then exited.

The grandmother met me at the door. I went to show her my ID card but she said it wasn't necessary. She said she knew that I was coming over to visit and that she recognized my voice. We talked for a good spell while we waited on Ronika to return home from school. She told me about how she had raised Ronika in the absence of her mother, a drug addict, and her son, who did not seem to have the time to raise his daughter. Only when she had heart problems and was hospitalized, did she have to turn Ronika over to the care of one of her daughters, Tasha Clarkson. Now Ronika had returned full circle, was the way she put it.

Fifteen minutes after my arrival, a car pulled up to the front of the property and Ronika was let out. She was an attractive young lady with a serious disposition. When we were introduced by her grandmother, she appeared lukewarm but friendly, not hostile. When I got the opportunity to talk to her alone, she was more relaxed and more opened with me. She told me she was alright being here with her grandmother but she wished that she could be with her father. That wasn't possible at this time because he was a migrant farm worker and he lived in a migrant commune. This wasn't a place or setting for a vibrant young teenager where men lived and worked, then drank and gambled to pass the time away.

After wrapping up my visit with Ronika, I headed for home. I was tired and I needed rest. After what I had gone through today, I had no clue what tomorrow would bring.

The following day, we received some sad news. One of our drivers, Jane, loss her husband the evening before. He was walking the dog on the beach, just around the corner from where they lived, and had a massive heart attack. He was a retired navy man and they had purchased their home years earlier after his navy career. There was an outpouring of sympathy, condolences, and emotional support from the staff. Jane was good people and everyone felt bad for her. To lose a loved one unexpectedly was unimaginable, especially when you had planned on spending the rest of your life with them.

That Friday I attended the funeral over on Anastasia Island at a Catholic Church there. Afterwards, we assembled at Jane's home to console her and have refreshments. During my visit, she took Phoebe and I, and a few others, to the spot where her husband had collapsed and died. A wreath marked the place along with flowers.

Death, it was something all of us would have to come face to face with one day.

Chapter 9

*T*wo weeks later, Karen summoned me into her office for the second time that week, this time to discuss a case that was being transferred to me. It was the Tiffany Boxer case. Tiffany was a twenty-four year old Black mother who lived with her mother in Hastings, Florida. She had three young children who had been placed with a relative caregiver with the court's approval. Tiffany was known to be promiscuous and she loved having affairs with older married men, I was told, and warned. Black men, it was emphasized. I was even advised never to be alone in her company. I took all of this in but said nothing. It was almost as if I had no say in whether or not this young seductress could have her way with me.

More interestingly, I pondered why they were going extra on the warnings since it was apparent to me that I fit the bill perfectly, as far as what type of man this woman was attracted to, according to them. It almost felt like a setup to me. But I decided to give my overseers the benefit of the doubt. I could not fathom why they would have it in for me. Besides, I was never the paranoid type unless I was given a good reason to be. But in all honesty, couldn't they have just assigned this case to a female if she was that much of a seductress and a threat to me? I thought. I mean, this would have been the way to go if they really had my interest at heart.

With the case file in hand, I returned to my desk and opened it and read through it. The following information is what I garnished from my reading: the child, D'Antonio Thompson, was hospitalized on August 25, 2004 weighing 4.69 kgm (approximately 10 lbs.) At birth the child weighed 3.22kgm (or 7lbs. 1oz.). The child was hospitalized due to failure to thrive and gained significant weight during his hospitalization. The failure to thrive was not believed to be due to medical reasons and was believed to be due to inadequate nutrition.

Upon further investigation, the Department of Children and Families found that the child had been admitted to Shands Jacksonville Pediatric Intensive Care Unit due to failure to thrive. Pediatrician Marcus Tony, M.D. revised his original finding of failure to thrive r/o metabolic cause to child neglect causing failure to thrive. The child was also examined by Dr. McCormick of the Child Protection Team who concurred with the finding of child neglect causing failure to thrive.

Prior to the child's admittance to the hospital it was established that no medical care was ever sought for the child. The last recorded doctor's visit was on 06/27/04 at which time the child received inoculations. The child was seen by a WIC nutritionist on 04/18/04. The reason the mother gave for the child not gaining weight was that he was born premature. As discovered earlier, the Health Department records indicated the child weighed 7lbs. 1 ounce at birth.

The children were subsequently removed from the mother's custody on August 21, 2004 and placed in foster care. On August 22, 2004 the Shelter Order was granted and the children were court ordered into foster care. The Department of Children and Families was given discretion to place the children with an approved relative upon completion of a positive home study. The children were placed with Andrea Kingston, paternal aunt of one of Tiffany's daughters. From what I read, Tiffany wanted her children back and appeared to be working on her case plan. That's where I came in.

That afternoon, I tidied up my cubicle area, flipped off my under cabinet light, and headed out to do a few home visits. My first visit was to see Deidra and Deon Elders, Ambers other two children, one she had with Don Juan Elders. Both were in a foster care home. After that visit I did one more in the area before heading over to Hastings, Florida to meet this vivacious and viviparous young mother named Tiffany Boxer, aka the manslayer, the home wrecker, perhaps a Nubian seductress reincarnated. Two minutes into my drive I was thinking no way this young girl could be all of that. No way!

The first stop I made in the small town of Hastings was at Mrs. Andrea Kingston's home, the caregiver with whom the children had been placed. She was a charming Black woman in her mid-forties. She had a southern folksy way about her and a southern friendly smile. We had met before during a conference convened by my agency about this case and the principals involved in it. This occurred when Phoebe was Tiffany's caseworker, just before my co-worker left the agency. Actually, this was why the case was transferred to me.

Mrs. Knight was active in the community. She lived in a home not too far from a house that had been remodeled by a popular home renovation television show the year before. She lived in a single family site built home in a predominantly Black neighborhood. Though this was a low income area, she had an attractive garden, one that was manicured and pleasing to the eye. We talked and while there I met the children who had been placed in her care. They were all under six years of age. Andrea briefed me on her nephew's past involvement with Tiffany and told me some things about her other relationships. Much of it was scandalous in nature and nothing I had asked to hear. But it gave me more insight on this young mother, and if not totally true and accurate, it clued me in on how others perceived her. After I checked out the living area and other spaces, I went on my way. My next stop, the Tiffany Boxer residence. Well, actually her mother's house.

Ms. Sandra Boxer, Tiffany's mother, greeted me at the door. She and Tiffany's father had never married nor ever lived together according to the notes I read in the case file. Ms. Boxer appeared to be one of those women who dressed to the nines every time she left the house. She was wearing a touch of makeup including lipstick. Her fingernails were painted and her hair styled in a curly Afro. She was wearing a tight form fitting skirt, smoke colored stockings, and an ankle bracelet.

I introduced myself and showed her my ID. Like so many other homes I had visited for the first time, she said she knew who I was and did not need for me to show her my identification. She asked me inside. I followed. She said that she was on her way out but that Tiffany was there.

Once we entered the living room area, Ms. Boxer invited me to take a seat on the recliner while she summoned Tiffany. I took up her offer and sat down as I watched her disappear inside of an adjacent room. When she reappeared, she told me that her daughter would be with me shortly. With that, Ms. Boxer bade me goodbye and was on her way out the door to make her rounds. So much for not being left alone with Tiffany.

As I waited on her, I looked about the area to see if there were any family pictures in view. There were some but they were of much younger children. While sitting I envisioned what a young mother, who started having children at age fourteen, then at age sixteen, and then seventeen, would look like. From her case files I knew that several of the fathers were twelve to fourteen years older than she was at the time she got pregnant. And though each child had a different father, there was a toss-up between two men who she felt could have been the father of her second child. Why a DNA test was never done, I don't know. But her promiscuous ways did not stop with these four men. From what I had heard, there were many more lovers out there she had entertained. I was certain that a young girl, with this much worldly experience, and childrearing, must have looked literally worn from the stress of raising three children no matter how much makeup she put on. But then again, from what I had read in the case file, her children were practically raised by others.

There was no reason for me to ponder this matter any longer. Tiffany Boxer had just made her appearance. To my surprise, she was as stunning and as attractive as everyone had said she was. If ever there was a Black Barbie Doll in the flesh, she personified it. She was wearing a brown leopard skin pattern scarf around her head, a blouse that had the first three buttons unfastened, which exposed ample cleavage, and she was wearing tight designer's jeans. She had a softness and sensuousness beyond her years. For five or six seconds, I found myself mesmerized by this young woman. But after that, I snapped back into professional mode and got down to the business at hand.

"Hello, I'm Carl Benjamin," I said, extending my hand.

"I guess you know who I am," she cooed. "If not, I'm Tiffany. Tiffany Boxer."

"It's good to meet you. May I?" I asked, looking back at the recliner.

"Sure," she said as she signaled for me to reclaim my seat. She sat down across from me and crossed her legs.

"I understand that you are interested in getting your children back," I began.

"Yes, I am," she replied. "Frankly, I don't know why they took my children from me in the first place. I mean, they claimed that I wasn't feeding them properly but that was nothing more than a lie."

"You're saying that these people are just full of rubbish, to put it mildly," I said.

"That's what I am saying," she retorted calmly.

"But your newborn was placed back in the hospital because of malnutrition, am I right?"

"I tried to tell those people at DCF that it was the baby formula I was giving him and since that time he's been given a new formula and now he's thriving."

"What about the fact that you did not take the child to the doctor to see what was wrong, when your son wasn't gaining weight?"

"I did take him to a doctor and was told that my son was alright and for me to try another brand of formula," she quipped. "I think it was a neighbor of mine who called in a false report on me saying that I wasn't taking care of my children."

"Listen, I am not here to interrogate you," I said leaning forward. "I just wanted to hear your side of the story and from your lips." Almost immediately, I chided myself subconsciously for my poor choice of words. I should have ended my statement at *'your side of the story, leaving the lips part of it out.'* Anyway, it was all for naught. Tiffany conducted herself in a ladylike manner the entire time I was there. She sat poised and regal like, though relaxed. Perhaps she was more the Nubian Queen than a seductress. That I still did not know. What I did know was that as we talked, never once did she toss a flirtatious gaze my way or deviate from the conversation I was there to have with her. Matter of fact, she was a woman of few words. But she managed to get to the point with what words she did speak. Brevity became her, I must admit. And because I came there with no preconceived notions about her, only what others had told me, I cannot say that I was totally surprised by her mature conduct. But I was.

I closed out my visit by going over her case plan with her and handing her my business card. I left the premise after that. On the way home I got a call from Roxanne. She told me that Aaron had been arrested for discharging his shotgun that night when confronted by a group of neighbors. He was charged with assault with a deadly weapon and reckless endangerment. Currently, he was out on bail, she told me. I told her that I would stop by the following day to talk with him.

Fridays were days we all loved in this business. With the weekend upon us, it meant a couple days off to get away, relax, and recharge our batteries. But we had to make it through the day first. Today was no different. With one exception, I spent the better part of the morning immersed in paperwork. I had an ESI staffing earlier that morning over at the Lightner Building for a new case I had just gotten the day before. The case name was Erica Tappers. Erica was a *'sweet'* sixteen year old who was two months away from her seventeenth birthday. From what I had read in the case file, her life had been anything but sweet. There was a time when sweet sixteen year old girls, those of social class, even those regardless of their social class, were introduced to the world's community through a pageantry-like forum known as a debutante ball. Like many great traditions that had faded into obscurity, this young debutante never had a chance at a traditional family upbringing. Her father and mother were not together, and had not been for most of her life. With only one parent in close proximity, she found herself fighting, with all that she had, for her mother's love and affection, yes...but most of all, for her mother's time. You see, mom was a busy woman. She worked at a Sony's Barbeque restaurant on US1 and on her off time, spent quality time with her boyfriend. It is this boyfriend Erica found herself competing with for her mother's time and attention. The relationship between mother and daughter was a contentious one. Better put, they just did not see eye to eye on things.

Mother eventually placed Erica in the custody of her grandparents but after a point in time, the arrangement became problematic. The grandparents worked long hours at a local restaurant. Not only that, they did not possess any legal paperwork showing that they were legally responsible for her. They could take her to the hospital but they were not privy to any personal medical information on their granddaughter. She could bring home participation forms from school but they had no legal authority to sign off on them. At some point in time, an alert teacher, or staff member, at Erica's high school called the abuse hotline. After a department investigation, her mother decided it was better for Erica to go into state custody because she couldn't find the time or the interest to be a parent. The case was labeled abandonment and Erica was placed in foster care. I would meet with her before the end of the day.

Since Phoebe's departure, I generally ate lunch alone. There was one other co-worker I went to lunch with on occasions, a young blonde named Jaime. In her mid-twenties, she had a slight resemblance to Christina Aguilera. Whenever we went out to lunch to one of the local restaurant establishments, we'd get our share of looks, I noticed over time. Personally, I brushed it off as nothing more than the fact that she did look like a celebrity. I would find it troubling to think that in this day and age, a Black man and a Caucasian woman would get such stares because of their skin color. In time, Jamie left the agency too. So, once again, I took off to find a place to eat in solitary. For a job that employed so many people, I'm talking people I interacted with on a daily basis; it got pretty lonely around lunch time.

Chapter 10

Erica was as sweet as you'd expect any sixteen year old debutante to be. But unlike most anointed debutantes, there was a sadness to her that should not have been there, especially for a young girl going through the various stages of adolescence. Without the proper love and guidance, this period often proved to be a challenging phase, and a troublesome one, as well, for any child, male or female. But to be shunned by one's parents and placed in the care of complete strangers had to affect a person emotionally. I knew of no one who did not have a need or desire to be loved and cherished. But not to be wanted, and abandoned, now that was some heavy emotional baggage to leave at the feet of a sixteen year old.

Erica was in a temporary placement just on the opposite side of the health department called Child Preservation. Though it was within walking distance, I decided to drive around the complex to it. Once I was allowed entrance, I introduced myself to her. Though troubled inside, I soon learned that along with her affable smile, she had strong survival instincts. That would prove to be a great attribute and asset for her growing up in the foster care system. We talked for about thirty minutes and then I departed but not before I promised to pick her up the following Monday so that we could go to her grandparent's house and get some of her clothing and personal effects. I took my camera, which I had in my hand, and snapped a picture of her for her case file.

My next stop was going to be at Aaron's and Roxanne's place on the Island. Out on bail, Aaron was awaiting trial sometime in the near future. When that would happen was anyone's guess. Along with the charges that I was told about by Roxanne the evening before, Aaron was also charged with disturbing the peace. I told him to keep me informed on any developments in the case. I also told him that a child protective investigator would probably be talking to him soon. This pronouncement seemed to unsettle him. But I told him that it was routine for law enforcement to contact the Department whenever a child was associated with any criminal act or perceived criminal act. While there I took an updated picture of Isaiah and departed.

On the way home, I stopped at the Peterson residence to check on John. I arrived there twenty minutes later to find a less than chipper boy. When I talked to him he said that he was still waiting for a visit with his mother. I told him that I had left several messages with his mother for her to call me back so that we could set up a visit but I had not heard back from her.

"When was the last time you talked to your mother?" I asked him as his grandparents sat quietly nearby.

"About a week ago," he said, after giving it some thought. "She told me then that she was going to call you but I guess she didn't find the time to do so."

"I'm sure there's a good reason why she hasn't called me yet," I assured him. "When you hear from your mother again, just make sure that she has my phone number."

"I gave it to her the last time we spoke," he quipped.

"He gets this way whenever his mother promises to do something but doesn't follow through with it," Harriett injected.

"Well, here," I said passing my business card for James to take. "This is one of my new business cards and it has both my office number and cell phone number on it. Make sure she gets both numbers, okay."

"I will," he responded as he seemed to return to his normal self.

"Have you added anything to your railroad project since my last visit?" I asked.

"Not much, but a few things," he chirped. "Want to see what I added?"

"Sure," I said, rising up.

His grandfather Fred lifted himself up out of the chair and followed us into the other room where all of the train sets were located. James took pride in showing me the additions to his railroad community, which included a Post Office and an additional train station. Then it was Fred's turn to show me his additions across the room in his railroad community. Harriett returned to working on a new dollhouse in the living room. Fifteen minutes later, James and I went outside to talk. I also took a photo of him for his file. This was something we were charged with doing every six months, and when we initially received a case, unless one had been taken and provided to us by the investigator. With camera, clipboard, and notepad in hand, I bade the family a pleasant weekend, climbed into the caddy I had christened the *Queen's Chariot*, and took off for home.

I spent the weekend relaxing and working on one of my novels. It was an intense and drawn out process but I loved to write stories. It was one form of escapism, one might say. As I often told people who asked why I loved writing, when you're writing, you can be anyone, go anywhere, be with anyone, fall in love with anyone, and dictate the outcome. That's why I loved to write.

Saturday Cynthia and I headed up to Jacksonville to attend a computer and electronics show. I usually bought parts for my computer at these events and other accessories. It was also an opportunity to see what was new in the market.

After the show we ate dinner at a nearby Applebee's, drove around for a while, then returned to the new home she had purchased in Palatka. Before that, she lived in East Palatka with her parents.

After our outing, I headed home. Certain individuals and their psychic abilities never failed to impress me but Renée topped the list with her eerie propensity to call me after I had spent time in Cynthia's company. Like clockwork, I heard from her the following morning. She was still up in Alaska visiting with her son.

"Hello, Renée," I answered casually, the phone was on speaker.

"Carl, sweetheart," she replied. "How are you? I was just thinking about you."

"So what was it that you were thinking about when you were thinking about me?"

"I was thinking about how you were doing and were you still roaming around the roads of, at least, five counties saving children."

"I am not saving children Renée. I'm just doing my job. Anyway, what if I were out there saving children. What's wrong with that?" I demanded to know.

"What's wrong?" she echoed. "I'll tell you what's wrong, Carl. You do not seem to have time for a serious commitment. That's what's wrong. And that's what went wrong with us."

"Well, you're wrong about that, Renée," I quipped, as I paced about my room holding the phone in one hand. "From the moment I first got involved with you I gave it my all. But that wasn't enough for you. You seemed to forget that I had a job, an important job, and it demanded a lot of my time."

"And left you little time for me, for us."

"Look, a man has to make a living," I snapped back, then after a moment, I soften my voice. "Please Renée, let's not argue, okay."

"Why do you sound so touchy and distant with me?"

"Renée, how long were we engaged?" I asked, sitting down on my office chair at my computer desk in my bedroom.

"Too long," was her short response.

"And how long have we've been apart?"

"Far too long," she answered. "So, what's your point?"

"My point is this, you have shown little interest in returning here," I began. "You see, my goal was always to try to work things out with you so that we could return to the way things were in the beginning. But I can see now that you truly have no interest in returning to me. Why you continue to call me puzzles me."

"I call you because I still worry about you, Carl, and I still care about you in a special way."

"Well, Renée, since you've been gone I met someone who I think truly cares about me and you know what? I think it's about time I spent more of my time getting to know her and less time thinking about how things could have been between us."

There was a pronounced pause before the voice on the other end of the phone came to life again. And when it did, it was in a condescending tone. "Carl, I can't say that I am not surprised because I am. But in all honesty, I knew it was only a matter of time before you threw yourself at the first woman who showed an interest in you."

"Look, I didn't throw myself at anyone, Renée. If anything, I've been ignoring Cynthia far too long and it's about time I did something about that."

"Don't think you're hurting my feelings," she snapped back. "But let's see how long Miss Cynthia puts up with your absences, your putting in late hours, your on-call schedule, and your middle of the night on-call crises. I give you two less than five months together."

"Look, if she cares about me the way I believe in my heart she does, she'll understand that I'm trying my best to do a job and do it the best way I know how to," I retorted.

"I don't believe this," Renée said incredulously. "You're in love with this Cynthia woman."

"Maybe I am and maybe she's in love with me," I retorted, grasping what Renée had just forced me to come to terms with. Was it true? Was I really in love with Cynthia?

"Well, good luck with that wishful thinking," Renée broke in. "I thought I could be just as understanding about your career choice myself but over time it became too much for me. I doubt she'll fare any better."

"Time will tell," I said in a firm voice.

"Listen, I wish you well, Carl, but you had better not get your hopes up too high," she cautioned me. "Love can be as elusive as one's pipedreams."

"Good night, Renée," I said, leaning back in my chair and staring out into space.

The following day, I headed up to Switzerland, Florida, just south of the Mandarin section of Jacksonville and spent the day with my friend and computer partner in crime, Jim Messick. While there we repaired a few computers I had brought along, Cynthia's was one of them, and while we worked, a NASCAR race played in the background on his new HD 42" flat screen television. This was our hobby. All I asked for, from those who sought our services, was a few dollars to cover the cost of my gas over to Jim's place, if the person could afford it. If they could not afford gas money, no big deal. I still drove the 50 miles to visit with Jim and work on the computer. Nearly all of the problems were software related. A lot of them suffered from computer viruses. Sometimes we'd find the problem in less than thirty minutes. Other times it took us hours of troubleshooting before we'd figure out what the problem was.

Later that evening I piled the repaired computers in the backseat of my car, climbed into the front seat, and took off for Putnam County. I would return them to their owners the following week.

On the way back I stopped by Cynthia's place in Palatka to return her computer. We talked, ate something she had cooked earlier, and talked some more. The subject then turned to cars.

"You know, I was just about to leave to head over to the carwash to wash my car when you pulled up," she said, as she repeatedly ran a comb through one side of her hair in a slow teasing motion.

"I didn't know that Cynthia."

"Oh, that's alright," she said. "I am still thinking about going over there to wash it. Believe me, it needs it."

"Mine needs a wash as well," I added, as I watched her turn her comb and her attention to the other side of her head. There was just something sensuous about watching her comb her hair. Then a thought seemed to occur to her.

Placing the comb down, she leaned forward on the sofa and said, "Listen, how about the two of us going over to Dairy Queen and getting something nice and cold to eat or drink, like ice cream or milkshakes, then we can go down by the riverfront to watch the boats sail by as we eat our dessert and then go and wash out cars."

"Sounds like a plan to me," I smiled, reaching over and helping her up off of the sofa.

"Let me go get a few things and then you can follow me, or I can follow you, over to Dairy Queen."

I watched in silence as she took off for her bedroom.

Arriving at Dairy Queen, we purchased milkshakes and drove our cars down to the riverfront. I got out of mine and sat down next to her inside of her car. In near silence, we devoured our dessert with our eager mouths and each other with our eyes. Every so often we'd tear our gaze away from one another to watch a passing speedboat or barge in the river.

Fifteen minutes later, we were on our way to the car wash. Once there we cleaned and vacuumed the inside of her Nissan first, then we went to work on my Cadillac. Afterwards, we drove both cars into adjacent bays and washed them, one at a time, while we worked as a team. One finished, we walked around both cars for a quick appraisal. Pleased, we high-fived one another, hugged, then headed off in different directions.

Monday I returned to work. Like many others, I was of the opinion that Mondays should be eliminated as a work day. The thought of working a four day work week sound cogent to me. I worked a four day schedule, ever so often, while serving in the navy. Hell, I was already putting in ten to twelve hour days in this business. As I tried to tell people, this was an emotionally charged field and a time consuming one. Caseworkers got burned out in this business, some sooner than others. It was often a thankless job where one mistake or an oversight could get you fired, or in a worst case scenario, cost a child their life. At this point, we're talking serious jail time. In light of this, the pressure to perform and stay on top of things remained great, sometimes it was overwhelming. People needed time off to exhale and regain their bearing. A weekend just didn't get it. But that was all we had to work with other than the option of putting in for leave. There just had to be a better way of getting this job done without stressing people out. But until that way was found, the battle to impact some child's life in a positive way waged on.

As I was walking through the conference room, I peered outside the glass door and saw Karen and Allison and Mike assembled down near the parking lot area standing and talking. Because of Mike's wide grin and animated gestures, I knew that they were not talking about anything serious so I decided to join them momentarily.

"How's it going Carl?" Karen asked me with her doe-like brown eyes. "Are we overworking you yet?"

"I'm doing fine, I imagine," I replied. "But thanks for asking."

"I'm just kidding," she said, her mouth breaking into a tight grin.

"Have you gotten the chance to meet Tiffany Boxer yet," Mike asked. He was one of her former caseworkers before he got promoted.

"Yes, I've met her," I answered, leveling my eyes on Mike.

"She's a hottie, huh," Karen said sporting her patented grin a second time.

"She's an attractive young mother," I answered, wondering all along where this conversation was going.

"She tried to seduce you, yet?" Karen laughed, throwing a quick glance and wink in Mike's and Allison's direction.

"Actually, she was quite the consummate mature young lady," I answered, apparently to their surprise.

"Well, that's a change up," Mike acknowledged. "Every time I turned around I was hearing about her exploits with men, many of them married."

"That may be true," I said with a confident smile, then continued. "But in my presence, she conducted herself like a refined young lady."

"Well, perhaps there's hope for her yet," Allison said smiling.

For the next couple of minutes the group got serious and talked about the Isaiah Hanson/Aaron Hanson case and the shooting incident he was involved in. Karen said that she already knew that Aaron was going to be told that he could not be around the child until the court said otherwise. It would come down to whether or not the mother wanted to be with Aaron or her son. We all agreed that more than likely, Roxanne would remain with her son knowing that with Aaron facing a trial he might end up in jail. She had her mother she could move in with along with her son. It was the only viable option for Roxanne. Besides, her mother already had custody of Roxanne's sister's daughter so there would be no need for a home study because one had been recently conducted and approved by the court. We'd just have to do the usual paperwork and submit it to the court.

Before we finished talking about the Hanson case, Mike and Allison broke in to say that they were heading off to eat lunch and do a few other things. That left Karen and I to talk.

Turning to me, she said, "Who's up in Alaska that you've been talking too? Is it business or personal?"

Taken aback at first by her question, it quickly dawned on me what she was talking about.

"Oh, that," I chuckled. "My former fiancée is visiting there with her son. Why, I have an abundance of free minutes every month."

"I know but it wouldn't look good if we got audited," she said. "So, just keep it strictly business from this point on. You know what I mean."

"Yeah, I do in a way," I retorted drily. "God, you mean to tell me that after all we go through as caseworkers, we cannot make a personal call on our job issued cellphones using the free minutes?"

"Nope," was her firm response.

"I imagine I'll be buying myself a phone later today," I said in exasperation.

"You don't have your own personal phone, I gather."

"No, I've always used my job issued cellphone, even when I worked in Daytona Beach," I said.

"Well, it's really not a big deal. From I see, this was the only number you've called."

"I have a landline phone at home I do most of my talking on. It's just that my ex is now four hours behind our time and it's easier for her to catch up with me while I am at work."

Easing her expression, Karen broke into a soft smile. Patting me gently on the arm, she said, "Come on, Carl. Let's go back inside before the place falls apart."

Walking up the concrete walkway we made our way to the conference room entrance. As I opened the door, Karen decided she was going to have a quick smoke. I entered the building without her.

After lunch I returned to the office to finish a case plan I had been working on before heading out to see Erica. Signing out, I made my way to the Queen's Chariot, cranked her up, turned the air-conditioner on full blast, donned my shades, then drove off to my next adventure.

That drive and that adventure began and ended less than a minute later as I parked the caddy on the other side of the complex where Erica was still temporarily holed up at until they found a more permanent placement for her at a foster care group home.

Though we had met the Friday before and she was polite and affable throughout my visit, I had yet to break the ice with her. That would take some time, though. But I was confident that I could get her to become at ease with me and share with me what was really going on in her head. Some workers never break the ice with their young clients. As a result, the child never opens up to them, and why should they when there's no bond or trust that exists between them and their caseworkers. I've always felt that as a professional, if I was ever going to have an impact or any success with a person, I had to cultivate a level of trust and mutual understanding with them. It's a fine line because of potential emotional attachments that can develop but it is an art that needed to be taught, if ever it could be taught. Otherwise, these children are forever deprived of having any memory or any semblance of a caring relationship and grow up with an emotional emptiness or detachment few of us ever want to know or experience.

I rang the doorbell and waited for someone to come and let me inside. A small glass porthole built into the door gave me a clear view of the full length of the corridor inside. Within a minute, a staff member appeared in the causeway and promptly approached the door. After I showed my ID and told them who I was there to see I was allowed entry.

Erica was seated in a room with three or four other girls watching television when I peered inside. She managed a trace of a smile when she spied me, then stood up. I signed her out then we headed for the car. I had a MapQuest printout of her grandmother's address just in case I needed it, but I didn't need it. Erica was able to direct me there on her own recognizance.

We parked the car in front of the gated property and waited. Her grandmother was supposed to meet us there after work. While we waited we engaged in small talk but there was still a barrier there, some hesitation on her part to fully engage me. But it was only our second meeting. There was no rush, though. Erica was going to be in the system until she turned 18. I could wait.

After thirty minutes there was still no sign of grandma or grandpa. Forty minutes later, I took off. She wanted me to take her to her grandparent's job but I felt it was too far away and it was getting late in the day. I had a few home visits I needed to get started with. So I told her we would try again the following day. I returned her to Child Preservation then began my home visits.

Half past five that evening, as I made my way towards Flagler Estates, I got a call from James Peterson's mother, Maureen Barnett. It was the first time we spoke to one another. For a while I was beginning to wonder if she really wanted her son back. Apparently, she did. As she spoke I made note that she had one of those deep sultry voices, much like actresses Lauren Bacall and Kathleen Turner. After she asked me a few questions about her case plan and I answered them, we managed to narrow down a date and time for a supervised family visit. I told her that I would get back with her after I talked to Fred and Harriett about their schedule.

Arriving at my first home visit, I thanked her for calling then hung up. This being the first of five visits I would attempt, I was in for a long night.

Chapter 11

Because I worked late the night before I came into the office around 9:30 AM the following morning. I was prepared to update a few of my case files and work on my mileage sheet and my time sheet. Before I could settle down in my chair, I was told that I needed to call Family Preservation about Erica. So I did. Apparently, she had taken ill and needed to be taken to the hospital. Withdrawing her file, I made a copy of the court order showing that we had child protective custody of Erica and I made a copy of her social security card. I grabbed a few other things during the process, signed out, and headed over to Family Preservation to pick Erica up.

I found her in the same room I had the day before, but this time she wasn't watching television. She was lying down on the sofa in the room by herself. The other girls had gone off to attend school.

"Erica, wake up. Your caseworker is here," the staff member announced softly as she shook my under the weather charge gently on her shoulder.

Erica stirred and glanced upward.

"Good morning Erica," I said as she sat up slowly. "How are you feeling?"

"Not too good," she said, her face a mask of pain.

"What's hurting you?" I asked her.

Grimacing, she mumbled something but it wasn't clear.

"Erica, you need to tell Mr. Carl what's bothering you, honey," the staff member coaxed her. "And try to speak clearly."

"My stomach hurts," she managed to say with some clarity.

"She's been complaining all morning, I was told after I arrived this morning," the staff member revealed.

"Okay, Erica," I said. "I'm going to take you over to Flagler Hospital to see what's wrong. Do you need any help getting up?"

She shook her head no. Rising up, she balanced herself in place and once she was steady she walked along side of me out of the room and slowly down the long corridor. She looked like someone who had not slept in three or four days.

Normally I parked the Cadillac in a parking space but today I parked in front of the entrance so that Erica would not have far to walk. After all, when I arrived I did not know what to expect.

It was on the cool side that morning and as I unlocked the car door, I saw her hugging herself. Every few seconds she'd shiver slightly. On the front seat lay a thick Temple University sweat shirt that I carried around for office visits that were extremely cold. I offered it to her to put on to keep warm but she politely declined. Opening the rear door, I had her sit in the rear of the car.

Flagler Hospital was less than two blocks away. I checked her in at the front desk which was positioned center of the lobby and to the far side of the room. The air conditioner seemed to be operating on full arctic blast. At some point, as we patiently waited, I got very cold. Erica was seated next to me, though more in a laying position than a straight up position, and she was shivering.

"Listen Erica," I said looking over at her, "I'm cold and I am going to go to the car and get a jacket. You want to reconsider my earlier offer to wear my sweat shirt?"

"Yeah, I'm cold, too," she said, letting out a yawn.

"Okay, I'll be back."

Outside it was beginning to warm up and frankly, if I could have conducted my business with that hospital from outside, I would have. That's how cold it was inside.

Returning minutes later, I handed Erica the sweat shirt, which she promptly put on. I was wearing my sports jacket and was feeling a lot warmer. While she was content to close her eyes and drift off, I watched the morning news show on the large flat screen television a few feet away. Actually, it was watching me more than I was watching it.

The receptionist finally called Erica's name over the PA system and the two of us stood up went over to her. A hospital assistant greeted us and led us into a room where we were seated. A nurse entered the space a minute later to take Erica's vitals.

"Good morning," the nurse said to us in greeting.

"Good morning," both Erica and I replied.

"Are you her father?" she asked me.

"I'm from child protective services," I said. "I'm actually her caseworker."

"I see, so what's ailing you Erica?" she said.

"I've been having some serious pain inside of my stomach since early this morning," she answered.

"Are you on any medications?" the nurse asked.

"No."

"Are you allergic to any foods?"

"Not that I know of."

The nurse positioned Erica's extended arm to have her blood pressure taken. A smaller handheld device was placed in her ear to record her internal temperature. Next, she was weighed.

Sensing that the nurse might need to ask Erica a few more questions on a more personal level, specifically pertaining to female issues, I asked her to summon me after she had finished her preliminary examination. Standing up, I returned to the lobby. Less than ten minutes later, I was recalled to the triage area.

"She has an elevated temperature and acute pain in her stomach area. I need you to see one of the accounts receptionists and provide them with Erica's Medicaid information. After that you can return to the lobby. A doctor will see her soon."

Erica returned to the sofa in the lobby while I took care of the business end of her visit. Shortly after I returned to the lobby, Erica was called in to see the doctor. I did not go with her but I did ask to be appraised by the doctor before he or she had completed their examination. Then I waited.

Fifteen minutes later I was escorted to the doctor's office where I was told that Erica had a urinary tract infection. The doctor gave me a couple of prescriptions to have filled and said that should clear it up inside of a week. There was no need for a return visit unless her infection did not clear up.

Leaving the hospital, we headed over to a CVS pharmacy to have her prescription filled. They told us it should be ready in an hour. Since we were only a block away from my office, we returned there. Allison, my acting supervisor, and Karen, our program manager, talked with Erica briefly to see how she was doing before she was shown a small and quiet reception room with a sofa in it where she could lay down. I returned to my cubicle to get some paperwork done.

Before leaving an hour later to pick up Erica's prescription, Allison told me that they had found a group home to place Erica in but it would be another hour or two before the paperwork would be ready. I told them that I was going to pick up the prescriptions and take Erica to get some lunch afterwards. I found Erica fast asleep on the sofa in the reception room and woke her up. I told her that the agency had found her a group home to move into later that afternoon. She seemed pleased.

"After we pick up my prescriptions, can we get something to eat," she said. "I didn't eat much for breakfast and I'm hungry."

"That's two of us," I said with a light chuckle. "Sure, we can get something to eat after we pick up your meds."

We waited approximately fifteen additional minutes once we arrived at CVS but we used that time to browse the store. I thumbed through a couple of magazines on the magazine rack. Erica glossed over a few fashion articles.

Once we concluded our business there, she took her medication right away. She chased the pills with a bottle of water I had purchased inside of CVS.

Returning to the caddy, we took off for lunch. This time she sat in the front next to me. She appeared to be more spirited, and livelier.

"Did you have any particular place in mind to eat?" I asked.

"Hey, could we eat at the restaurant my grandparents work at?" she asked.

"Where is that?"

"You know where Denny's restaurant is on US1?"

"Yes," I said, as I passed a slow SUV.

"Well, it's just down from that restaurant and hotel. It's not far."

"Sure, why not," I said. Actually, this would give me an opportunity to meet someone in her family for the first time.

We arrived at the restaurant fifteen minutes later. Since we had arrived just before the lunch hour rush, there were only three or four couples seated inside talking and eating. The workers there were obviously aware of who Erica was and greeted her enthusiastically. Within seconds, she disappeared into the kitchen area. I sat down at a table and waited. Several minutes later she reappeared with her grandparents in tow. We were introduced, traded pleasantries, and talked briefly. Unfortunately for us, they were preparing for the lunch hour rush and could not stay long to talk. They did give me permission to take Erica over to their house to retrieve some of her clothing and personal items. Then they returned to the kitchen. For a few minutes we looked over the menu.

A gum chewing waitress in her mid-forties eventually came over and took our order. Within twelve minutes, we were eating our lunch. Erica and I talked and ate and talked some more. And the more we talked, the more relaxed she became. Finally, I thought, she was opening up her mind and sharing her thoughts to me. We talked about school, life in general, her friends, her family, and her future.

After we emptied our plates, I wiped my mouth with a napkin and asked for the bill. I was ready to go and wanted to pay for our meals. The waitress smiled and told us that lunch was on the house. Pleasantly surprised, both Erica and I thanked her. Before leaving I left her a generous tip. Erica caught up to me after she said goodbye to her relatives. Climbing into my car, we drove off. Her visit with her grandparents obviously lifted her spirits. If only they could have cared for her.

We returned to her grandparents' home and parked my car outside of the gated entrance. Two large dogs, and they must have weighed at least sixty pounds each, approached the gate wagging their tails but did not bark. While Erica opened the gate and went inside and petted the canines, I got out and opened the trunk of the car and rearranged a few things. After greeting the dogs, Erica entered the home and when she reemerged a short while later, she was carrying articles of clothing. It wasn't much.

"Is that it?" I said looking at the bundle in her arms.

"That's all that's in the house," she answered, handing me the clothing. "They packed the rest of my things in the shed."

"How much more do you have?" I asked as I placed what she had given me inside the back seat of the car.

"I don't know," she said. "But I can go and see."

"Okay," I replied checking to see what time it was on my cellphone.

I watched as she reentered the property, the dogs trotting a short distance behind. After I had rearranged the trunk, I stood there for a while, then turned around. She was making her way towards me carrying a large bloated dark green trash bag. Handing me the bag of clothing, I placed them in the trunk of the car.

"Is that it?" I asked.

"There' two more bags like this and my stereo and some stuff animals," she replied.

Stuffed animals, I mused. "Look, I'll go with you and help you carry them," I said, following her.

"They won't bite," she assured me after seeing my apprehension when one of the dogs got too close for comfort and started sniffing my legs.

Erica opened the wooden door of the shed and we stepped into the cool darkness within. Erica reached for a light switch and the space brightened up. She warned me to be on the lookout for snakes and field mice. Copperheads she stressed.

Inside of this good size shed was lawn equipment tool boxes, and numerous cardboard boxes, most of them taped shut. To the far side of the cluttered space were three large bags stacked, side by side, on a wooden bench. All three were similar to the one she had brought out to the car. Nearby sat a bloated bag of stuffed animals. She pointed out the two bags that contained her personal items and we headed towards them. As we walked, little puffs of dust arose from every footfall. The dirt on the floor had long ago turned to powder.

Fortunately, we managed to make it over to her belongings without seeing any snakes, though we heard what we thought was a mouse milling about in an area nearby but mountains of stacked newspapers and several boxes blocked our view. Grabbing her belongings, we returned to the car with them.

While I placed them away in the trunk of the car she returned to the shed to retrieve her small stereo components and two pairs of shoes. After two more trips to the shed, I loaded the rest of her things then entered my car. Walking over to the gate, Erica reached over it and gave the dogs a hearty pat on the head and a warm goodbye. After she made sure the gate was secured, we took off for her new home.

During our drive, Erica shut her eyes and fell asleep. The medication she had taken earlier was probably sapping her energy, as well as the workout she just had moving her belongings. I drove the next eight miles listening to my favorite smooth jazz station, though at a low volume.

Once there, it took close to an hour to get Erica moved in and all of the paperwork processed. I gave the staff member, whose name was Dawn, the low down on Erica's visit to the hospital and told her about her medication. I found Erica in her new room and told her I was about to head out. I had one more home visit I wanted to make. She thanked me for taking her to the hospital and for the use of my sweat shirt, which she returned to me.

"It was my pleasure," I said, then turned to leave.

"Have a good day," she said softly.

"You too," I said in acknowledgement but without looking back.

On the way to Interlachen, I stopped off in Hastings to visit with Ronika and her grandmother. I found Ronika holed up in her bedroom at the far end of the single wide mobile home when I arrived. She looked bored and somewhat lonely. I might even add mildly depressed. As I looked around, it was apparent to me that there was really nothing for her to do there but homework and watch television. Teenaged girls were generally outgoing. Being cooped up in a small house with no one her age she could relate to didn't help matters any. Her grandmother, Lynn Sue Dobson, was in the kitchen frying chicken wings. And boy did they smell good. She offered me one but I politely declined. However, she insisted so I relented and took one and bit into one of the tastiest piece of chicken this side of Kentucky. While she wrapped up things in the kitchen area, Ronika and I went outside on the screened in porch to talk.

"How are you doing?" I asked, facing her.

"I'm okay," she said half-heartily.

"If you ask me, you look bored," I said boldly.

"Yeah, I'm that too," she admitted with a sweet smile.

"Do you get to go places," I asked.

"Sometimes," she replied. "My grandmother loves to go fishing so I go with her and her friends when they go. I also get to visit with my aunt that I used to stay with every once in a while."

"What about hanging out with your friends?"

"No, I don't get to do that much."

"You have a boyfriend?"

"Sort of," she said sheepishly.

"What do you mean sort of?"

"Well, we're kind'a seeing one another on the side but his mother doesn't like me."

"Do you get to see him much?"

"In school and we talk on the phone."

"I see," I murmured. "Do you have any relatives around your age you get to see often?"

"Just my cousin who lives in Palatka with her brother and mother. My aunt's name is Wanda. You know her?"

"No, I can't say that I do."

"Aren't you from Palatka?" she asked me.

"I'm from Interlachen," I answered.

"You live way out there," she quipped.

"Yes, I do, and I like it out there," I answered. "Listen, when was the last time you saw your mother or father? I was just wondering if you ever get to spend time with either one of them. I know they are not together but do they make an effort to see you or call you?"

"My father works all of the time and when he's off, he's gambling or drinking or just hanging around the place he lives at with his farm worker buddies," she explained. "Now, my mother, I see her around town every couple of months. But no, she doesn't call or stop by to see me."

"Do you know where she lives?"

"No, not really. I do know that she's a drifter, that's all I say with certainty."

"You mean she goes from one place to another, much like a gypsy."

"You can say that."

Leaning back in the chair, I gazed over at Erica, thoughtfully, as I paused to absorb all that she had shared with me. By now her grandmother had appeared at the door entrance. She joined us on the porch where we talked some more.

An hour after my arrival, I took off for home. Ronika, though dearly loved by her grandmother, was as happy as a caged tiger, just plain miserable. But you could only do so much as a caseworker while they were in the care of their relatives. She did say they went fishing. How boring could that be?

Chapter 12

Amber Sawgrass stopped by to visit me the following day. She wanted to let me know that she was out of jail and ready to schedule a visit with the two children we had in foster care. As for her son Dennis, I reminded her that she was free to work out supervised visitation with his father, whose custody he had been placed in. After checking my schedule, I told her that I could arrange a visit the following day but that I would have to call her later with a time because I had to notify the foster care parents ahead of time. Though she was showing big time now, her pregnancy, that is, this did not prevent Amber from being flirtatious with me. But I took it all in stride. I had learned long before now how to deal with women much like her. Basically, I politely ignored her subtle come-ons.

That afternoon, I finally got to meet James Peterson's mother, Maureen Barnett. She stopped by the office so that she could follow me to the Dairy Queen restaurant nine miles south of the office where her son and his grandparents would meet us for the family visit. She had traveled down from Jacksonville.

Maureen, though a slightly overweight woman, still had enough of a shape that most men would find appealing. She had short and curly reddish brown hair and wore a solemn look. I introduced myself, gave her preliminary directions, in case she lost me along the way, then we got in our cars and took off.

James and his grandparents, Fred and Harriett, were already there waiting on us in the parking lot of the restaurant. James got out of the van and rushed his mother. The two hugged and exchanges pleasantries. The grandparents entered the restaurant. I followed James and his mother inside. We all ordered something to eat and drink. The grandparents sat a good distance away from where James and his mother sat, but that wasn't a big surprise. I sat a few tables over from mother and son so that they could have their semi-private time together, though I was close enough to observe their interactions. From time to time, I'd go over and chat with the grandparents.

An hour later, mother and son embraced and said goodbye. James appeared teary-eyed but managed to maintain his composure. Before leaving the premises, we decided on the next date for a visit. Once that was settled, we all got into our vehicles and drove off. Based on what I had heard about their previous visits and the tensions involved, I was happy to get through this visit without any flare-ups between mom and the grandparents. Everyone acted surprisingly civil.

Today was Veteran's Day and Cynthia and I decided to head over to St Augustine to look for some curtains for her house. While there we stopped at a JC Penny's department store and browsed through their drapery section. Our efforts were for naught. They didn't have the size or the color she was looking for. Since we were in the area, we decided to head over to the historic district for lunch. An up scaled restaurant named Harry's was where we dined at. This was a place a couple could easily walk out of there with a forty dollar tab for lunch. But I loved to eat and socialize at the same time and the food, the atmosphere, and the service was worth every penny spent. Since I rarely got to eat at such places during working hours, I relished the opportunity when it came around, especially when Cynthia was at my side. I was midway through eating my Lobster Newburg meal when it began to thunder. Lightning flashed in brief intervals minutes later. The loud clapping of thunder seemed to unnerve her at times. In a short while, the downpour came and with a vengeance.

After we were through eating, it was still raining, but the thunder and lightning had subsided.

"What do you want to do?" I asked her. "Wait until it stops raining or we do we take a chance at getting wet as we make our way back to your car."

Exhaling, she gave me a thoughtful gaze then said, "I think we ought to take our chances and try to get back to my car." Her Nissan was parked across from the Lightner Museum five blocks away.

"Okay," I said, going into my pants pocket for my debit card. After paying the bill and leaving a tip, we headed out.

With me on point, we made our way through the downpour hugging the walls of the businesses we passed by. We were like infantrymen making our way from one building to the next. Every other business, we paused in their covered entrance to dry off before we bolted again to the next foyer. Sometimes when I looked back, Cynthia was behind me. Other times she was one building behind me. I'd wait until she caught up with me before I proceeded on.

Dashing across King Street, we made our way over to the Casa Monica Hotel, the luxury hotel I longed to patronize one day for a two or three day leisure visit. Once inside their grand lobby area, we headed straight to their luxury restrooms where we dried off our faces with freshly folded towels. Amazingly, their restrooms did not look like your typical restrooms. These were several notches above your average restroom, even those found at luxury hotels at Disney World.

Meeting up in the lobby, we made our way over to the exit facing the Lightner Museum. When we arrived in the area it was fairly sunny outside. Now the skies above were ominous and overcast. What we saw next was unlike anything either one of us had ever witness before…anywhere! The street below from where we stood marveling at the forces of nature had turned into a river of rushing water. There was no other way to get to the other side of the street but through this impromptu waterway. We were going to get wet, no matter what.

Stepping outside, we huddled closed together under a narrow covering, rain pouring down just inches from our faces. Several other people joined us. Still in awe of what we were witnessing, I looked over at Cynthia and she looked back at me.

"Listen, if you want me to, I'll go and get the car and drive it over here for you to get in," I said, my eye and eyelashes dripping with drops of water. "That way you will not get too drenched."

She appeared to ponder my offer before saying, "Thanks but that's okay."

"Cynthia, it's no problem," I assured her.

"That's okay," she said, glancing out at the rushing waterway just a few feet away. "I think we ought to keep going."

"Are you sure?" I asked, gazing over at her lovely face.

"Yes. I figure that since we're this close, we might as well walk the rest of the way. We're going to get soaked, no matter what," she seemed to reason aloud as she turned her gaze in my direction.

For a second or two we stood there gazing at one another. Her searching eyes stirred something deep inside of me. There was something sensuous about her brown eyes, her wet face and her quiet calm.

"You ready to do this?" I finally said in a last ditched effort to gauge whether or not she wanted to remain steadfast in her resolve.

"Yes, we might as well get this over with," she said, taking a gulp of air. "There's no way we are going to avoid getting our feet soaked and the rest of us drenched. So let's just go." I could see she was not enjoying this. Me, I thought it was kind'a neat.

On point again, I bolted down the concrete stairs and into the street. Cynthia followed a short distance behind me. I knew the water had risen significantly but I was stunned by how deep it was once I found myself in it. The water level rose far above my ankles, and by at least three inches. The very instant we stepped down into the water, our shoes were thoroughly soaked and so were my socks. Cynthia wasn't faring any better. Her face and hair were getting drenched as well. On top of that, the rushing water was extremely cold.

Once we made it to the other side of the Lightner Museum, there was one more obstacle we had to traverse. This street was flooded as well. It looked very much like the rapids you'd find on the Colorado River. By now, we were both soaked from head to toe and no longer running, having resigned ourselves to our inevitable reality. We were already drenched and running was not going to change anything. Instead, we walked, though rapidly, down the long stretch of sidewalk.

Minutes later, we arrived at the parking lot then made a final mad dash to her car, water splashing about whenever we'd step into a puddle. Once inside we took several minutes to wind down, dry off, and catch our breath. Cynthia started up the car and turned on the heat to warm us up. The outside temperature must have dropped twenty degrees in the span of thirty-five minutes. It took us that long to get to her car. Normally, this was a twelve minute walk.

"I cannot believe how much water this storm has produced," Cynthia exclaimed, her hair stringy, much like a wet mop. "I have never seen anything like this before."

"It always floods in this area when there's a downpour," I told her. "I don't think they have ever invested in good drainage in this area. County commissioners have no desire to tear up the streets to install runoff piping. It would affect business too much."

"Well, they need to do something about this," she insisted. "I have no desire to come back down here when it is raining this hard."

"I thought it was kind of fun, myself," I said chuckling. "Actually, I enjoyed going through this with you. It's a memory I'll never forget for as long as I live, I'll say that much."

"Well, you've got a point there," she admitted. "I'll never forget this either. I just don't want to get wet like this again. I could end up catching a cold and so could you."

Turning towards her, I smiled and said, "Cynthia, I would have gotten the car for you and drove it back to the hotel and you would have been spared getting drenched."

"I wished I had taken you up on your offer now," she said, her face breaking into a warm smile.

"Well, why didn't you let me get it?" I asked curiously.

"I guess I'm just not used to having someone around to do special things like that for me," she said in earnest as she tended to her hair.

I said nothing as I stared at her side profile. Her words touched me in a surprising way. It was a poignant moment for me and one that gave me additional insight into the psyche of this most interesting of women. More than ever, I found myself wanting to doing a lot more for her than just retrieving her car.

Training bored me for the most part but I knew that it was a necessary evil, if I'm allowed to put it in those terms. They lasted too long and often turned into meetings that resembled grip sessions. But today's training had to do with hurricane preparations. This training was interesting and held my interest.

After training, a group of us went out to lunch. It was one of those rare get-togethers where we all came together without any cliques or skullduggery involved.

Once back in the office, I worked on my time sheet and mileage. It was a time consuming and burdensome process. It took hours to calculate weeks and months of travel miles and what was due me and we did this all manually. Sure, in a perfect world I'd fill out the form every day as not to get behind but I did not exist in a perfect world. I decided I would have to develop a spreadsheet that would do the calculation automatically for both.

After I had enough of number crunching, I decided it was time to take a ride over to see Erica. I spent a half hour with her and while there, helped her with a homework assignment she was having difficulty with. After that I was scheduled for a family visit with Amber and her two little ones, Deon and Deidra.

That afternoon, I picked up the Sawgrass children at Brandt's Daycare and transported them to the site of the family visit. The visit went off well. We met at the playground adjacent to the public library on US1 and just a block down from SR 16. For a change Amber was more absorbed with another entity than me. She doted on her two children as you would expect any mother to. Deidra appeared to recognize her mother though it had been a couple of months since her mother saw her. The baby probably did not have a clue who was holding him.

After the Sawgrass visit, I returned the children to their foster care home. Since I was in the area I stopped over Roxanne Henri's mother's house, who lived less than a mile away, to check on her and her son. Aaron was allowed supervised visits conducted by the maternal grandmother so I wasn't surprised to see him there. He shared with me his concern about going to prison for the shooting incident. After discussions with his attorney he said he was not optimistic about avoiding jail time. But he remained hopeful. While there he and Roxanne informed me that she was pregnant.

I returned home that evening and for a change, did not bring carryout with me. I selected a microwave meal from the freezer and put it on after I ate a salad I had made the day before. Later, I sat at my computer and started work on a spreadsheet program to help make my life a lot easier when it came to calculating my mileage and tabulating my time sheets.

The office was rather noisy the following day. One of the workers had a family visit scheduled at the office with a mother and her four young children, all four within running, jumping, playing, and talking aloud age. To top it off, the mother wasn't scheduled to show up for another thirty minutes. Too me, office visits were too sterile and clinical for my taste. Besides, caseworkers were very busy people and any opportunity they got to do some work in the office was time they utilized to the fullest, well, most of them, to get caught up on work they had fallen behind on. Distractions always made the task that more difficult. Besides, I preferred the natural surroundings of a playground, if the children were of age to appreciate and enjoy playing with other children. I also met at the local library for such visitations. That's why most of us conducted our family visits somewhere other than the office. With true grit, along with a sympathetic disposition, I managed to endure this sudden imposition and complete a predisposition study I had been working on.

After lunch, I drove over to St Augustine High School to drop off some court related documents they needed for Erica to complete her enrollment there. Her school records had already been transferred there by her previous school. While there, I met with and spoke to two other teenagers in my caseload, then departed. From there I headed over to the county jail to visit with Elyse, who was still holed up there. Amber and Donna had been released weeks before. She had only a few more days before her own release and was anxious to get out. Usually reserved and thoughtful, she appeared more relaxed as her release date grew nearer. We talked about her case plan and family visits. I also emphasized that she needed to start thinking about staying clean, if she had not already. Her daughters needed her and they needed her in her right mind. After that visit, I took off to pick Erica up. She had a counseling session scheduled at the mental health department, just across the hall from my agency. In this business, we played chauffeur as well as case managers. I also had a clothing allowance check I needed to give to the house parent for Erica. Normally this process went through the normal channels but since this was an emergency clothing allowance, I would deliver it in person.

It was still wet outside when I got in my car. There had been a light shower an hour earlier. Cranking up my car engine, I took off. Because of the overcast sky, I had no need of my sunglasses.

Traffic was light on US1. It usually was after the lunch hour rush. I arrived at the foster care group home where Erica was holed up at, just off of SR 16, about ten minutes before she and the other young boarders returned from school. While I waited, I talked to a staff member. I also had her show me Erica's room. I wanted to see where they finally placed her and also to see if she was a good steward.

"She's really a very neat girl," the house mother said as she showed me the side of the room that Erica occupied. "But then again, she doesn't have a lot of things here yet."

"What about those bags of clothing we brought over?" I asked.

"Most of what she had was winter wear. We stored them away for her."

"I see," I said as we left the room and returned to the main lobby. "Anyway, I have good news for you and for Erica. I have a clothing allowance check for her." With that, I opened my long notepad and pulled out the check I had tucked away inside the pages and handed it to the house mother.

"Good! She could use some more clothes," the staff member said. "We gave her some surplus articles of clothing we had in storage but there wasn't much that fit her. And she needed more shoes. Now we can go out and get her these things. Thank you."

"You're welcomed," I said as we both turned to see who was entering the space from outside. Three girls rushed inside playfully but were told to walk by another staff member arriving in the area from another part of the house. The three of them came to a screeching halt. Another girl entering inside spied me and approached me.

"Hello, sir. Are you Erica Tapper's caseworker?" she asked me with a girlish smile.

"Yes, I am," I answered.

"She said she thought that was your car outside," the girl said. "She's on her way. She had to go back on the bus to see if she had left a book on the seat."

"Thank you," I said as I looked beyond her shoulder to observe Erica walking in. Her face seemed to light up when she saw me.

"Hello Carl," she said with a lazy smile. "How long you've been waiting?"

"Not long," I answered.

"Hello Mrs. Sharon," she said to the house mother.

"Hello Erica," Mrs. Sharon replied as the two embraced. "As you can see, this one loves to be hugged," she said grinning, as she gave Erica a warm motherly gaze.

The two released each other.

"You're here to take me to my counseling session?"

"You got it," I replied.

"Okay, I'll be ready after I take my things to my room," she said. "I hope Mrs. Sharon didn't show you where I sleep."

"She did," I smiled.

"Gosh, you probably think I'm a neat freak or some'n," she said feinting a frown.

"Actually, you're in good company," I replied. "I'm one."

She smiled on that statement.

Within minutes we made our way back to my office and her counseling session. While she was over at mental health, I returned to my desk to take care of a few things. There was always something to do.

Forty minutes later I walked over to Elizabeth's office, just down the hall, to see how she was doing and to see if she had any candy in her candy dish. By now, Elizabeth was a seasoned supervisor and an excellent one. We talked for a while until I decided it was time to check to see if Erica was ready to go home. And yes, I got that piece of candy as well.

Along the way I stopped at a Target store and purchased a 'to-go' cellphone. I did not want to sign on to any two year contract or have to remember to pay a monthly bill that was due. So I went this route. I made one more stop to get some gas. While I took care of the gas, Erica, who was more familiar with this technology than I, set my ring tone and also picked out a scenic wallpaper for my phone display. It was a horizon that had a beautiful sunset image on it. Before we took off, she showed me how to work a few other settings on my phone. Once we had my phone up and running, I took off.

A week later, as I sat at my desk talking to a Guardian ad Litem volunteer about a case we were both involved with, my acting supervisor, Allison called saying she needed to see me in her office, though there wasn't any rush. Just the same, I wrapped up my conversation with Mrs. Mildred Castle and found my way over to Allison's office.

"Whatz up?" I asked as I leaned against a file cabinet to the front right side of her desk, my right arm resting on top of it.

"Ronika Dobson's grandmother is back in the hospital with heart issues," she said. "I think she might have had a heart attack, but I'm not sure.

"Anyway, Ronika has an aunt that came forward who will take her in but it's not the aunt that had custody of her before. It's the older aunt this time."

"Where does this aunt live?" I asked.

"In Palatka somewhere," Allison said. "I sent the address to you in an email, so check your email, okay."

"I was in court for another case so I had the shelter change taken care of then. All you have to do is check on Ronika before you knock off from work today and meet with the aunt."

"Will do," I said.

That afternoon, I headed over to visit Dennis Bowls Jr. and his father, Dennis Bowls Sr., who was now living in a single wide less than two miles south of the office on US1. He and his former girlfriend had a falling out and he had to move out. So I was here to do a home study.

Dad answered the door shirtless and ushered me inside.

"How's it going?" I asked.

"Not bad," he said. "I have to get this air-conditioner checked out by the landlord. As you can tell, it's pretty warm in here."

"Yes, it is," I replied as I looked about the place for the first time. "When is your landlord going to fix it?"

"He's got an air-conditioner man that's going to come out and check on it tomorrow," Dennis Sr. answered as he offered me a seat on the sofa.

"So, where's Dennis Jr.?" I asked, as I readied my home study form to write on.

"Look," he said, his voice now slightly high pitched and defensive in tone, "I know I'm supposed to supervise his visits with his mother but since today is her birthday, I thought I'd let him spend a little time with her. Anyway, they should be returning any minute now."

Whatever I was doing at the time, I paused and gave him a pointed stare. "You mean to tell me that your son is with his mother Amber? Dennis, that's an outright and direct violation of a court order. Man, you could end up back in jail because of this."

"I didn't know it would lead to all of this," his muttered, his voice now nervous in tone.

"What were you thinking, guy?" I asked, my voice steady and firm.

"Like I said, it was his mother's birthday and I just thought that it was no big deal, that's all."

"Well, it is a big deal," I answered. "You don't go around disobeying a court order. Think about it now. If something happened to your son right now and the court found out that you allowed his mother to have custody of him when she only has supervised visits, man, you'd be skinned alive by the judge."

"Listen, the judge doesn't have to know, now does he?" he asked as he tried to get a fix on how I was going to play this.

Whatever he was thinking, or hoping, I was playing this strictly by the book. "Dennis, you put yourself in a bad position. That's not going to happen with me. I'll have to let my supervisor know, and the court, that you allowed your son to spend time with his mother while she was unsupervised. That's the bottom line."

"I guess you have to do what you have to do," he murmured.

"You got that right," I said. "Now, we might as well get this home study out of the way, just by chance the judge lets you get by with this one. But I wouldn't bank on it."

I went ahead and conducted the home study. By the time I completed it, some forty minutes later, mom and son had yet to return. I waited another fifteen minutes, then left. Before leaving, I told dad that as soon as Dennis returned home I wanted him to call me and I wanted to hear his son's voice. Other than that, I'd make sure this information made its way through the necessary channels the following morning. If I knew Judge Alexander, he was going to blow a gasket once he learned about this father's total disregard for his court orders. Personally, I was perplexed. Amber was cute and all but not worth going to jail over, I remembered thinking.

On my way home, I found Ronika's aunt's house just off of Alabama and St Johns Avenue in Palatka, Florida. The aunt, Wanda Brookings, though married, lived in the single family home with her two teenaged son and daughter. Her husband had suffered a stroke months earlier and had been hospitalized. He was now in recuperating in an assistant living facility somewhere in Gainesville, Florida. Outside of the house was a large sign made out of wood that had the name of her business on it. Apparently, the aunt ran a licensed daycare center out of her home.

After I explained my role to the aunt and her role, as well, she brought up the issue of relative caregiver funds. When her sister had custody of Ronika, she recalled her sibling getting money to provide Ronika with personal items and clothing. I assured the aunt that I would make sure the paperwork on the relative caregiver funds would be processed the next day. After that, the aunt and I finished our conversation. I then asked if I could speak to Ronika outside in private, as I always did with the children in my caseload who were old enough to have a sensible conversation. Though I did not need her permission to talk to Ronika in private, I asked just out of courtesy. Ronika and I exited the home and walked a short distance away from the entrance.

"So, how do you feel about being here?" I asked her.

"It's alright," she said somewhat solemnly.

"Well, at least you'll have your cousins around to keep you company," I noted with a smile.

"That part is true," she said drily, her eyes averted momentarily.

"Do you and your aunt get along?"

"Not really," she admitted.

"Is she strict or something?"

"Very strict," Ronika snapped back.

"I see," I murmured.

"I mean, it's not really that bad, she just kind of goes overboard sometimes with her rules," Ronika said.

"What kind of rules?" I asked.

"We have to get up at five o'clock every morning and pray, for one. And we are not allowed to take phone calls after seven in the evening. Add to that, we are not allowed to watch certain television shows, you know, that kind of stuff. I'm tell'n you, she treats me like I am a little kid or something."

"Well, Ronika, we don't have too many options in your case as far as suitable placements. And as bad as you think you may have it here, I don't think you want to end up in foster care," I said. "Just the same, I'm going to monitor your stay here just to make sure everything is on the up and up, okay?"

"That would be good," she replied, her arms now crossed at chest level.

"Look, how are you doing on clothes?" I asked.

"That's something I wanted to talk to you about," she replied gazing up at me. "I still have a lot of clothes over at my grandmother's house in Hastings. Is there some way you can take me over there to pick them up?"

"Sure," I quipped. "You have some way of getting inside the house?"

"Not really, but I don't have to," she answered. "Everything that was in the house, what little that was, I packed up and is already here. Everything else is in bags on the screened in porch at the back of the house."

"Your aunt won't take you to pick up your things?"

"She been saying that she will but she hasn't yet," Ronika said. "Besides, she has to wait until all of the children she provides daycare for are picked up by their parents. By then she says she's too tired."

"I imagine I can take you over there tomorrow after you get out of school, how's that?" I asked.

Ronika smiled and said, "That will work."

For a young girl who recently turned seventeen, Ronika was mature beyond her age. Though she appeared to be a quiet wholesome young girl, I had read her case file when I was assigned it months earlier and knew that she was alleged to be sexually active. Being raised and shuffled between various family members probably contributed to her growing up a lot faster than other children normally would. All of us have basic survival instincts within us when we are on our own, or feel like we're on our own. It was like my Tiffany Boxer case, where nearly everyone associated with it told me that she was this and she was that and I did not see any of those things when she was in my presence. I wondered if this was Ronika's case...bad press.

After taking a photo of her, I bade her goodnight and headed towards my car.

"Please, don't forget me tomorrow, Mr. Carl," she said waving.

"I won't," I replied, glancing back. "Just be ready."

"I will."

Chapter 13

Things had calmed down between the Browning family and the complex's office manager, and thankfully. Mrs. Browning told me that she had gone over to the office days earlier and had a long civil discussion with the manager and the two were able to resolve their differences. The boys were permitted back in the game room and allowed to use the computer lab again. They were also allowed back in the swimming pool. I asked her what it was that she said to change the heart and mind of the manager. She said...

"I had a heart to heart talk with the manager about my grandsons and I admitted to her that they could be a little hardheaded and rambunctious at times, but I also told her that I found it hard to believe that my grandsons were responsible for everything that went wrong in that complex," Mrs. Browning explained to me. "Then I asked her to pray with me."

I nodded my head. "Aaah, so that's how she came about having a change of heart," I uttered.

"As they say, God works in mysterious ways," she said with her patented smile. "Since our talk, I have not had one complaint out of that office. Not one."

"Well, that's great," I said, as we sat at the dining room table waiting on the grands to return home from school. When they started filing in, I took pictures of all of those who were present during my visit. I'd have to get the other's pictures another day, I told her. I left shortly after talking to her young brood. As I drove south on US1, it did not escape me that Mrs. Browning looked a lot weaker from the cancer that was destroying her from inside. It wasn't a matter of if, but when she would succumb to her illness. All along, I pondered the fate of these children once she did succumb. Their father and mother were scheduled to be released from jail in a couple of months but I wasn't so sure grandma would be around then. I could only hope and pray that she would be.

My next stop was a visit with John Steele at his foster care home over on the island. Paul, his foster care parent was an architect and actually designed his beautiful home he and his wife and their two dogs lived in. Paul offered me a cold beverage and the two of us sat down in the dining room area and talked as we waited for John to arrive from school. He said that John was a good boy but seemed to be struggling with his school work. He said that he had to make sure John let he and his wife know about every homework assignment he had because in the past, they discovered that he was not doing his assignments. Other than that, he was allowed to talk with his sisters and his grandmother and mom over the phone whenever he wanted to before eight in the evening. He said that they had done some things together but John was prone to be reserve and distance at times.

It wasn't long before John arrived home. He was carrying a backpack and wearing a gentle smile when our eyes met. He had obviously seen my car parked outside on the way in and knew that I was here for a visit.

After he put his school books and other gear away, we went outside to talk. We stopped by my Cadillac and faced each other.

"So, how are things going for you here?" I asked.

"Okay," he said, his eyes glancing downward, not in a way one would when hiding something, perhaps a troubling thought, but more so because he was an outright shy boy.

"Is that all, just okay" I asked. "How do you feel about being here?"

"I like it," he said. "But I still wished that I was home with my family."

"Well, I understand that John, believe me," I said smiling.

"Am I going home any time soon?" he asked, looking up at me with curious eyes.

"Your mother is still working on her case plan and only after she has completed it will you be able to go home to her, as well as your sisters," I explained.

"How much does she have left to do?" he wanted to know.

"I'll have to check but not too much," I tried to convince him. The truth of the matter was that his mother wasn't doing much of anything with her case plan but I couldn't tell him that.

"Then hopefully I'll get to go home soon?"

"Let's keep our fingers crossed, okay," I said.

"I will."

"Okay," I replied. "Now, I need you to do something for me. Actually it's for you."

"What?"

"I need you to stay on top of your homework, okay?" I said, placing my arm on the roof of my car.

"I'll try," he said but not convincingly.

I looked at him and raised my eyebrows slightly but said nothing.

"It's just that my homework can be pretty hard at times."

"John, that's the time you need to let Mr. Paul and his wife, Mrs. Charlene, know that you need their help, okay?"

He nodded.

"Well, I have to be heading out," I told him as we walked back towards the house.

"When am I going to visit with my sisters and my grandmother and my mother again?"

"I believe we're getting together in another day or two. I have to check my calendar."

We returned inside of the house where I talked an additional ten minutes or more with both of John's foster care parents. I told them that I had encouraged John to seek their help whenever his school assignments got too difficult for him. After I had answered all of their questions, which were few, I told Paul that I'd see him at the next family visit. I thanked them both for the soft drink and departed.

Next, I drove over to Marge Hamilton's house off of SR-207 a quarter of a mile east of Wildwood Street in a community of high quality manufactured homes. I arrived there twenty minutes later. By now, she had asked for and was granted custody of John's little sister Shannon, with tacit approval of the children's family. What the family was most happy about was that all three sisters were together now in the same placement. When I arrived, the twins, Sherrie and Shelly, and little sister Shannon, were seated at the table waiting for dinner to be served. With the exception of little Shannon, the twins looked distance, almost sad. That began to make me percolate inside with anger from past injustices done to children who were helpless to do anything about their situation. For a while, Marge seemed to have changed her ways, especially after our talk a month earlier on what once appeared on the surface to be a rough and abrasive approach when disciplining the twins.

I was particularly interested in talking to the girls because of an incident that had reached the desk of Karen, my program manager. Apparently, someone in the mental health department, who was familiar with the case, the twins, and their foster care mother, Marge, was out shopping at Wal-Mart the night before and saw Marge yelling at, and manhandling, one of the twins as they waited in the checkout line.

Hearing this, I called and asked Marge about the incident. Not surprisingly, she denied that what she had been reported to have done was as bad as it had been reported. I wasn't so certain about her take on it having had witnessed her before get a little out of control. But if what was reported was true, and we had no reason to believe it was not, Marge had gone beyond the realm of self-control, she had become completely unhinged.

Marge was bringing out a casserole dish to place on the table and Shelly went to reach for something and Marge's respond was quick and sharp. She told Shelly to wait. The way she said it and the tone she used was hostile in nature. That really got my antenna up. The reality was this, if this woman was bold enough, or just plain ignorant enough, to act this way in my presence, a child protective service caseworker, how was she acting when I wasn't around.

I sat in the living room observing Marge's interaction with the children and waiting for the girls to finish their dinner. The twins hardly said a word throughout the meal. Shannon, whom Marge seemed to favor, seemed immune to the situation at hand involving her sisters. When Sherrie and Shelly got up from the table, they had only eaten three fourth of their meal. Marge happened to make a terse comment about that in a disgruntled tone of voice.

Shannon got to me before I could get to her sisters as she came running into my embrace. Scooping her up in my arms, I hugged and kissed her on her rosy cheek.

"Hi Carl," she said with a bubbly smile.

"Hello Shannon," I replied smiling. "And how are you doing today?"

"I'ma doing fine," she answered in broken English.

"Good," I said, easing her back down on her two little feet. "Listen, I need to talk with your sisters. I'll get back to you before I leave, okay?"

"Okay," she said with a wide Shirley Temple grin, dimples and all.

One by one I took Sherrie and Shelly aside and went outside to talk with them. I did not like what I was hearing. They told me about getting beaten and restricted to their rooms for hours on end. They told me about how she shouted at them all of the time and shook them violently. Inside my blood was near the boiling point. How could someone in a foster care position charged with helping these children, terrorize them? I pondered.

Enough was enough. Fortunately for these children, they had me to protect them. Once I sent Shelly back inside, I made four calls. First, I called Ronika to tell her that we'd have to get her personal items from her grandmother's house the next day. I explained to her that an emergency had come up. Though mildly disappointed, she was very understanding. The second call I made was to my supervisor. The third call was to our program manager. Her call was the same as mine...remove the children immediately. The fourth, and final, call was to the abuse hotline to report what I suspected and what the twins had shared with me.

Returning inside, I made the announcement to Marge that I was taking in my care and custody, all three children. I then explained to her why. I also reminded her of the discussion we had had on this same topic a month or two before. She was genuinely shocked and did not seem to grasp why I was removing the girls from her home. She just did not get it and that probably explained why she had continued on with this behavior after my initial warning.

After I packed what I could into the trunk of my car, as far as their clothing and toys, I made a call to their grandmother to see if she could take them in until we could get a new shelter order. I would process the original home study, which was less than three months old. Not having an extra bed in the house was one of the things that had prevented them from being granted custody of the children. They had that extra bed now. The children's legal father, who was once living with the children's mother at their grandmother's house, was no longer living there. Besides, like the children's mother, he was eventually allowed supervised visits by the court with his daughter Shannon and the other three children.

Within twenty minutes we were pulling onto their grandmother's property. Expecting our arrival, she greeted us at the door before I could turn the car engine off. The three girls exited the car and converged on the family matriarch like firemen called to the scene of a fire.

Grandma Lorraine and I talked in length about what had just happened and she found it hard to believe that Marge would do those things the girls had mentioned. Both she and Marge had struck up a friendship of sorts. But if came down to believing Marge or her grandchildren, she said it was going to be the grandchildren's word she was going to believe. Anyway, she was happy to have her family back in her care. Right now, though she had mixed feelings about Marge and her situation, having the grandchildren back was all that mattered to her now.

The following morning the updated home study was submitted to the court and the maternal grandmother was granted custody of the three girls. By the end of the week we would move to have John reunited with his siblings as well.

While in court, ti did not come as a surprise to me that Dennis Bowls Sr. was royally chewed out by Judge Alexander, and rightfully so, for allowing the child's mother, Amber, to have unsupervised visitation which was in direct violation of the court order. With his head hung low, the child's father stood there before the judge looking remorseful and dazed. Few could weather a serious ass chewing by Judge Alexander and walk away unfazed.

$\mathcal{I}$ spend the better part of the day getting Dennis placed in foster care. For a six year old, his rambunctious reputation had well preceded him. Having been in foster care before, every foster care parent was aware of him and his shenanigans and his bad temperament. The child was so special a case he had to be home schooled for a period of time due to his bi-polar diagnosis and his penchant for being aggressive and uncontrollable, along with having anti-social behavior and a lack of respect for authority figures. When the child was in Hastings Elementary School, he tried to stab his teacher with a knife.

The child was so off the chain that once, when left with his psychologist, during a session, he attempted to bite her, actually scratched and kicked her, and then pulled down his trousers and mooned her before farting loudly (flatulence, as the good doctor noted in her notes). This was a six year old child who weighed no more than forty-five pounds who was creating all of this havoc around his peers and adults, as well.

The one exception to his madness, I had discovered, was putting him in the company of a strong personality type who was in a position to bring dire consequences into the equation.

It was a warm day, not a hot autumn day, so I had the car windows lowered and the air conditioner turned off so that I could allow the breeze to flow through the interior of my car. After we found someone who would take Dennis in, which took every bit of five hours to find, I put him in the car and took off for his new placement. The agency was so desperate to find someone to take him in that they told the foster care mother they would pay her the maximum allowable payment above what she'd normally get, just to get her to take him.

As I drove west on SR-207, all seemed normal. We were actually having a pretty decent conversation about rap artists, which he seemed to know a lot about, when I caught him, out of the corner of my eye, grab something and quickly tossed it out of the window.

"Dennis, what did you just toss out of my window?" I asked.

Glancing back at me sheepishly he just smiled without uttering a word.

"Dennis, for the second time, what did you just toss out my car window?" I demanded to know this time.

The boy just continued to smile and what a devilish smile it was. Looking down I noticed that my ID badge was missing. It had been positioned on the car seat by my right leg. Thinking the unthinkable, I immediately slowed the car down.

"Dennis, did you just toss my ID badge outside of the car?"

The kid still refused to say anything about what he tossed out. Moving into the left lane I took the next turn off, made a U-turn, and headed back to the area I remembered the boy tossing an object out of the window. After another U-turn, I doubled back.

I drove as slowly as traffic would permit and when I saw an object that resembled my ID badge lying on the side of the curb, I stopped the car, got out of it, and retrieved it. At the next stop, I pulled the caddy over, parked it, and faced the child, who right now was nothing more than a spoiled brat in my eyes. The choice words I served him I will not repeat here, but I can say that none of it was vulgar and I didn't put my hands on him. But I did make it clear, in no uncertain term, that if he ever did that again, he was going out the window after it. I can happily say that we had a clear understanding from that point on since he never attempted a stunt like that again with me. Sometimes such pranksters needed to be called on their actions and in my estimation, there were times these rumbustious children needed and had to be reined in.

Unfortunately, society doesn't allow much latitude for men to be men, much like when I had my little tête à tête with Dennis after he tossed my badge. Reprimand was the term they used back in the day. You chastise someone child today and there's a lawsuit. And do not expect the state to back you up. Children can act out, cuss you out, and just plain show their rear ends out, at times, and there is little you can do, and they know this.

Fortunately, I had only two cases that involved an unruly child. But I was always quick to establish parameters with these difficult children and I knew how to be firm when the situation required a firm approach. Young children today were not being taught to respect others, especially their elders, since in my book respect has always been a two way street. Children these days were not getting this valuable lesson. In a lot of the cases, we could thank their parents for this. How sad.

Chapter 14

*R*onika appeared happy to see me. She looked prepared to do some serious hauling for she was wearing jeans and a plain blouse. Unlike her, I didn't know what to expect. Most of the moves I've made with other girls in my caseload did not require a lot of time or energy because they never had more than two or three large bags and perhaps a suitcase to their name. But because I arrived straight from my job, I was not dressed to do any serious moving. After I talked to her aunt briefly, Ronika and I took off for Hastings, the same small town I had passed on the way over from St Augustine to Palatka.

Going over to her grandmother's place was liken taking a mini vacation for Ronika from her sometimes strong-willed and slightly overbearing aunt. Joy sometimes came in small packages, they say. I say one should take it no matter what size it came in.

The house was locked up since her grandmother was still hospitalized. But the entrance to the rear screened in porch was unlocked. I followed in Ronika's wake as she led me to the back of the house, which was actually on my right side the way it was positioned on the property. In the corner of the screened in area were several swollen black trash bags that she said contained her clothing and other belongings. There were at least five or six large bags. But unlike the other girls I had transported in the past, Doniella B and Doniella D, Porsha, Briana, and Erica, to name a few, Ronika did not have a lot of stuffed animals.

After I dropped Ronika off at her aunt's house in Palatka and unloaded the car, I took off for home. That evening, I put the final touches on the two spreadsheets I had designed to manage my mileage and time sheets. I would give a demonstration of what they could do the following day at the job. I wanted to start using them in an official capacity as soon as possible. I also took time to soak my leg in an Epsom salt bath to ease the soreness from all of the lifting I had been doing lately on my injured knee and pain ridden lower back. Both I had injured and sought treatment for during my navy days.

A month later, after an exhaustive and thorough investigation by the state, Marge Hamilton finally had a hearing scheduled later that afternoon. At the hearing it would be determined whether or not she would be allowed to remain a foster care parent. I was called upon to be a witness for the state. I had no concerns about my involvement or actions in the case. All that happened and all that I had observed over the months had been documented. Still, it was thought-provoking and sad knowing that more than likely Marge was going to lose her foster care license. I'm sure she had good intentions but she just went about this the wrong way. My question remained this, how did she manage to make it through the screening process with her unsavory parenting skills?

The hearing was attended by me, a couple of supervisors and Karen, our program manager. There must have been thirty other people in attendance, as well.

Most of them I knew, the others I didn't. I was the third witness to testify. A representative for the state questioned me and then I was crossed examined by Marge's attorney. I told them of my concerns, what I knew, and about my early intervention months earlier with Marge. I shared with them what the girls had told me, as well as what I had personally observed. After fifteen minutes of questioning, I was dismissed. Before the day was through I'd learn that Marge lost her foster care license.

Though the children were now in the care of Lorraine, the children's mother, Alisha, disappeared from the scene shortly after the hearing. Word I had gotten from Lorraine was that Alisha had relocated to Texas with her new boyfriend. From what I understood, she was still married to little Shannon's father, Jeremy Jameson. Actually, Jeremy was more involved with the children than their mother. And three of the four were not his biological children. But I suspected that he was still very much in love with Alisha and was hoping and waiting for her to return to her senses, her family, and to him. In addition to this, I had never seen him or John have a cross word. The two got along great. It made me wonder if the initial report about him hurting John wasn't actually like he said it was, ruff play. I had two nephews, one eight years old and the other almost five. One day they were flipping one another and the youngest broke his arm. I say this to remind people that stuff happens.

After the hearing I readied myself to conduct a family visit with Amber, her son Dennis, and the two little ones, Deidra and Deon. We had decided to meet at the playground next to the public library. This was also the playground that had the carousel at one end of it. The Guardian ad Litem on the case had given me notice that she would be there too.

I grabbed two car seats, one for Deidra, a toddler, and one for Deon, the baby. I drove over to the Armstrong, an area west of St Augustine and centered near SR-207, to pick up Dennis at his foster care home. Next we went and picked up his siblings at their foster care home on the other side of town off of SR 16. We pulled up into the library parking lot as Mary, the Guardian ad Litem. Dennis was good about holding his younger sister's hand while I unstrapped Deon from the car seat. There were numerous children playing in the playground and riding the carousel. Mary and I, and the children, settled on a bench near the carousel and waited for mom. She arrived ten minutes later.

We greeted one another then Amber went over and retrieved Deon from Mary's arms, who had been holding him while I had held Deidra. Throughout the visit, Mary seemed to interrogate, and from what I witnessed, aggravate Amber. Other times it seemed as though she was nick picking her. Why, I could only guess? I was left to speculate that the two were from two completely different worlds and Mary, an educated and retired professional, did not think highly of Amber, a young mother who had not gone beyond the tenth grade. Amber was a product of living on the streets. She was not above working as a prostitute when it served her needs. She also used drugs. These were all of the things Mary looked down on and despised, it was apparent to me. I tried to referee the two but it was a hopeless cause. Mary would say something that pricked Amber and Amber would snap back with words that cut like a knife. Finally, I decided it was time to bring the visit to an end.

I talked to Mary in private and expressed my concerns about her attending future family visits involving Amber. To my complete surprise, the GAL apologized to Amber and myself for stirring up discord which resulted in their heated verbal exchange. Mary explained it by saying that she it was not her intent to get into a verbal confrontation with the mother but she could not help being judgmental towards the mother, who was verbal and defensive in her own comments. She said that it was no need to end the visit on her account but that she would go ahead and leave. I really didn't know what to say but I was happy that we had reached some sort of truce before the visit was over. Amber seemed willing to forgive and forget. She just wanted to spend time with her children. And frankly, that's why we were there in the first place.

After Mary left the premises, I held the baby while Amber and her older two children went for a couple of rides on the merry-g-round. Afterwards, we took the children inside of the library to use the restrooms. Amber decided to check out a few movies while we were there. Again, I sat holding Deon while she and Dennis and Deidra browsed through the library's DVD collection. At one point Dennis came over to me holding a 'slasher' movie his mother was going to check out for him.

"Do me a favor Dennis," I said to him. "Ask your mother if she could come here. I need to ask her something."

"Okay," he said taking off.

While I waited, I dried Deon's mouth area with a cloth because he was drooling again. Amber showed up a second later and lifted him up in her arms, to my relief.

"Yeah, what do you need?" she asked, with a flirtatious look and easy smile.

"Amber, what is going on inside your head?" I asked.

"What?"

"Tell me now, do you really think a Freddie Kruger movie is something six year old boys should be watching?"

"My son watches this stuff all of his lithe time," she shot back with a playful grin.

I shook my head in disbelief. *I can see why his mind was messed up*, I thought but said, "Amber, please try to find him something more age appropriate, will you?" I said. "You know, there's a company that makes great children's films, I'm told."

"And what company is that?" she asked, with an inquisitive gaze.

"It's called Walt Disney."

"Yeah, right," she chuckled and took off.

We left the library fifteen minutes later and thankfully, without any slasher movies. I took the younger two children home first then Dennis. Amber caught a ride with whoever dropped her off who had now returned to pick her up.

Before I knew it the Christmas holidays were upon us. I was entering my third year with the agency and as with any company or business, people come and people go. In the past three months we had a several new caseworkers added to replace those who had left the agency or took other positions within it. Replacing Tara was a young beauty named Kelly. She was probably her high's Prom Queen, with blonde hair, Barbie Doll looks, and all. How much experience she had as a caseworker I did not know. Then there was Wendy. She was a Nubian Princess and beauty in her own right. Sometime later four other Nubian princesses joined the team, Lajosha, Renee, Patricia, and Ashanta joined us as well.

By now I was bringing my manuscript in for Erin K. to read on her own time. She did clerical work for Maria, the head of mental health services. Erin had taken an interest in my writings and honored me by proof reading them. Earlier that week we had an influx of donated toys and bikes and electronics come in, including a number of cellphones for the teenagers. Every child in foster care was provided a generous amount of toys and other gifts. Some of the older teens got $50 gift cards.

The first batch of toys, electronics, bikes, and Christmas toys I got my hands on went to the Browning family. Next on my list were Sergio and James, then John, Shelly and Sherrie and little Shannon. With thirty-six children in my caseload, I took me nearly two weeks to deliver all of their gifts. The last two to get their Christmas things were Erica and Ronika.

Four days before the big event, I stopped by Ronika's aunt's house. Wanda, her aunt, greeted me and we talked. Ronika was not home, but out with her cousin visiting a friend. During my visit, Wanda told me that her husband had passed away a few days earlier. I offered her my condolences. She also told me that she was thinking about moving to Palm Coast once she got the insurance money from her husband's life insurance. But all of that was down the road, she said. Before leaving, I had her walk me out to the car. I was hoping that Ronika would have arrived during my visit so that I could have given her, her Christmas gifts in person. That's why I hung around for about twenty minutes. But after a point, I was ready to go home. Opening the trunk of the car, I handed her a bag and a suitcase full of gifts. One was a cellphone. I knew she would like that gift. Again, I extended my condolences, wished her a merry Christmas, and departed.

Penny stopped by to see me and wish me a merry Christmas. It had been a while since I last saw her. I told her that I was a little disappointed that she wasn't making a lot of progress with her case plan. She promised to get back in gear after the holidays. As magically as she had appeared, she disappeared. Never once did she mention her sons or the aunt she called mom while in my presence.

One of our new caseworkers was Kevin, a Black male whom you might say was of a different persuasion. Picking up babies and holding them just was not his thing. Kevin had apparently talked with the program manager, Karen, to ask if I could take over home visits for one of his little infants in Middleburg, Florida. The child was named Vanessa. A one year old, she was in a medical foster care setting. Being born with an undeveloped brain, something doctors attributed to her mother's heavy drug use, she was not expected to live beyond the age of two or three. As stated, Kevin did not care for handling babies or making that long trip to Middleburg when I lived just south of it, though it was some twenty miles. But I agreed to do his monthly visits.

Before signing off for the day, I left to visit Vanessa in Middleburg. It was a long ride but I got there inside of an hour. Since it was around four in the evening, traffic was heavy, especially because of the Christmas shopping that was going on.

The foster care mother, Mrs. Gloria Shaw, who had been expecting me, greeted me at the door. It was a lovely single family home that would easily appraise at $120,000. Without hesitation, she led me into the bedroom where Vanessa lay asleep. She was lying in a crib inside of her room that had medical equipment the likes you'd find in a hospital room. They were there to monitor her vitals and to keep her from dehydrating and to feed her. A tube from one machine was attached to her little arm. She looked so precious lying there in her pink dress. Mrs. Shaw told me that I could pick her up if I wanted to. It was time for her to change her anyway, she said.

Reaching over the side of the crib, I picked her up gently. If no one had told me that something was wrong with this baby I would have thought I was holding a normal baby. But sadly, there was something wrong, something very wrong. In the span of twenty seconds, as I held her close, I said a prayer on her behalf, my eyes growing moist, my heart growing heavy. I knew that this blessed child would probably not live pass the age of four. Why? I wanted to know from God. Why the young and helpless? Why this child?

I left but before I had driven off the property my eyes were red in color and quite misty. If only there was something I could have done, I thought. Miracle workers, where were they when you needed one?

I took a week off for the holidays. My most prized gift was that the agency had approved my spreadsheet programs, not just for my own use, but to be used agency wide. Now I wouldn't have to spend so much time during time sheets and mileage. A day into my leave, I returned to Philly for a wintery visit. It snowed, looked postcard beautiful, especially along the East River Drive near the Philadelphia Art Museum and Boat House Roll facing the Schuylkill River, then I was ready to return to Florida.

My first day back, I met Cynthia and gave her a belated Christmas present. She treated me to dinner as a gift.

Sitting side by side, we ate and somehow got into a light discussion about parenting and how many children were lacking it. We both agreed that the country's value system had deteriorated over the years and to a point it was not a big deal for men to bring a lot of children into the world, and with multiple women, and not be there to support them or give guidance to them. As for women, it was no longer a stigma to have a family with children who had two or three different last names amongst them. It was no longer a stigma to be uneducated or on public assistance any more. Morality and self-pride was a thing of the past, it seemed.

"Listen, what do you look for in a man, Cynthia?" I asked, leveling my eyes on hers.

"Well, I imagine the basic things most women would look for," she said.

"Like what?" I asked, stirring my straw in my drink.

"Like someone who is intelligent, ambitious, confident, clean, and God fearing," she countered, tossing me one of her thoughtful gazes.

"Clean?" I asked.

"What I guess I mean is someone who is well groomed and smells clean," she explained, taking a bite of savory shrimp. "Some guys, and women, do not have good hygiene."

"Anything else?" I asked, leaning back in my chair.

"I guess I'd like for him to be educated and business-minded to a degree."

"I guess that's it, huh," I said, blinking.

"I guess so."

"Hey, what about looks?" I quipped, tapping the table with my fingers. "Does he have to be attractive?"

"That he has to be, and he must be very masculine," she said taking another bite of shrimp.

"Masculine," I murmured back with a little more bass in my voice. "Sounds like you know what you want. And it ain't no wimp. Anyway, I was just wondering."

"Nothing's wrong with wondering," she replied, placing her hand on the table top, just inches from my hand.

"I guess you summed it up pretty well," I tacked on.

"It would also be nice if he was outgoing and quite handy around the house," she said with an infectious smile. "Now, what about you? What do you look for in a woman?"

"I look for a woman with beautiful brown eyes and a beautiful heart, not a perfect one but a loving one," I began.

"Sounds endearing," she said giving me another dose of those her doe-like brown eyes of hers. "What else, Mr. Romance Writer?"

"I just want someone who can be all of the wonderful things a man could ask for at least a couple of times a week, nothing more, nothing less," I replied.

"That doesn't sound like much," she said, taking a sip of her drink.

"It's not much but it's what I need," I replied.

"You sound more like a man of mystic riddles than poetry," she said, her eyes sparkling like miniature lanterns.

"I am neither a riddle nor a mystery but everything poetic," I came back with a mystical gaze.

"Okaay," she cooed, searching my eyes with hers.

I chuckled. "Listen, I'm just playing around."

"I'm not," she said as she leaned over and kissed me with pursed lips and closed eyes. God, her lips were moist and tender.

After that sweet broadside, I sat speechless as I trained my eyes on Cynthia, her sparkling brown eyes and soft inviting smile more enhanced than ever. The woman was intoxicating to my senses, much in the same manner as a goblet of fine wine. I knew there was an attraction there but I never suspected it being anything of this nature. And it wasn't because I didn't want her to feel these things for me. Perhaps it was because I had been preoccupied with my ex fiancée Renée returning to me to notice Cynthia's growing passion for me. With that one kiss, I felt like she had awakened something powerful inside of me. This was as poignant a moment I've found myself in a while. With my heart pounding madly inside me, I knew I would not be able to look at Cynthia in the same way from this point on.

Chapter 15

With the Christmas holidays behind us now, things finally settled down and returned to normal. Alyson Jenson, Sergio Labriano, Jr.'s mother, stopped by to provide me with information on her new job and to give me with an update on how things were going with her at school and with her son. As for the child's father, Sergio Sr., she told me that he was still behind bars.

Early that afternoon, I headed over to the foster care group home where Erica had been holed up at for the past couple of months. Because of overcrowding, she was being moved to another group home located somewhere in St Augustine Shores, a community of middle to upper class homes which consisted of spacious single family homes and a few upscale apartments, a convenience store, and an elementary school.

Erica greeted me with an enthusiastic smile. We went through our own specialized hand greeting, which included a the tapping and clapping of one another's hands with a combination of both closed fist and open hands, then a snapping of our fingers, with it all ending with a pointing gesture, as if to say to each other *'you got it!'* We hugged and then got down to the business of moving her. Once everything was in the car, she said her final goodbyes to her friends and staff members there and we took off.

Since I had not had lunch, and was starving, we stopped off at a McDonald's restaurant where I got something to eat and drink. Erica bought an ice cream cone while we were there.

Afterwards, we headed over to her new high school, Pedro Menendez, on SR-206, where she was going to be enrolled at.

When all was said and done, we got back in the car and headed over to her new group home. She seemed a little on the anxious side but that was to be expected. We found the place sixteen minutes later.

Unpacking her belongings, I sat down and filled out a mountain of paperwork that needed to be completed before I left. I talked to Erica briefly before leaving, then headed out to embark on a few home visits. The last visit I made that evening was at Ronika's aunt's house. She didn't seem to be in a good mood.

"So, how are things going with Ronika?" I asked Wanda.

"Not good," she said without giving it a thought, her expression soured. "Not good at all."

"Care to tell me about it?"

"Girls, they are just too much trouble," Wanda said, shaking her head side to side. "Listen, I went out to a meeting the other night and I told Ronika and Shakara, my daughter, that I did not want them to have any company over. I make it a habit of telling them that when I'm not around no one else should be here inside of my house, especially these fresh behind boys.

"Well, the following day, my son happened to slip up when I overheard him talking on the phone. Whoever he was talking to, he mentioned that Ronika and Shakara had two of their male friends over when I was gone and in their bedroom. In my house, mind you!"

"What did the girls have to say for themselves?" I asked.

"Nothing. Absolutely nothing," she quipped. "That's one reason why I shelled out all of that money to have a six foot fence put around my property. To keep those boys off of my property and away from my windows. God help me if one of these girls gets themselves pregnant. Then you'd want to take both of them away from me."

I shook my head but said nothing as I jotted a few things on my notepad.

"You know, I'll be glad when I move to Palm Coast."

"You're still planning to do that, uh?" I replied.

"The life insurance money finally came through," she answered, calming down. "Didn't you see my new car outside?"

"I saw a nice looking car out there but I thought you had company over."

"Naah, that's my new car. You want to see it?"

"Sure, why not," I said as we stood up.

Exiting the house through a side door we entered the covered carport where Wanda's new Pontiac Grand Prix was parked. She told me she traded her older car in.

"So, you're living large now, I see," I teased.

"The Lord has blessed me, that's all I'm going to say," she came back with a smile.

Ronika and her cousin Shakara showed up minutes after Wanda and I returned inside. After Ronika had settled in, I had her walk with me to my car so that we could talk in private.

"I hear that you got in a little trouble with you aunt recently," I said.

"I knew she was going to tell you that," Ronika quipped, fuming. "But it's not the way she probably told you."

"Did you have boys in your bedroom?"

"No, they were at the window, not in the room," she insisted.

"Well, your aunt seems to think that they were in your bedroom."

"No, they were at the bedroom window."

"So why were they on the property to begin with?"

"One was Shakara's boyfriend and the other guy was with him. He tried talking to me but I already have a boyfriend and I told him that."

"Yeah, you did mention that to me before," I said. "He lives in Palm Coast, right?"

Ronika nodded her head yes.

"I'm just wondering, how did you happen to meet your boyfriend when he lives down in Palm Coast and you live here?"

"His mother owns a beauty shop in East Palatka and he helps out there once in a while and that's how I got to meet him."

"I see," I murmured. "Have you've seen him lately?"

"A few days before Christmas when I met him at the Palatka Mall to get my Christmas present from him."

"I take it that he has a car or borrows his parent's car."

"He has his own car."

"I see," I murmured. "Speaking of Christmas gifts how did you like what I dropped off?"

"Oh, they were nice," she said as she zipped her coat all the way up. It was wintery outside and cold. "When did you bring them over?"

"Sometime before Christmas," I replied. "But you weren't here, as we both know."

"I do know that I was supposed to wait until Christmas Day to see what I had gotten but I couldn't wait so two days before Christmas, I opened them up to see what I had, then resealed them."

"Well, they were your gifts, after all," I said. "So, how did you like the cellphone?"

At that moment, Ronika gave me a puzzled look. "What cellphone?"

"What cellphone?" I echoed incredulously.

"I didn't see any cellphone for me in those gifts," she said.

"Are you sure?"

"I'm positive," she insisted.

I glanced towards the house momentarily than back at Ronika.

"So, I was supposed to get a cellphone," she said in disbelief. "What kind was it?"

"It was a to-go phone," I answered. "But I don't remember the brand."

"Did it come with minutes?"

"Yes, I gave your aunt a small gift wrapped package that had a $50 AT&T refill card inside."

Ronika stared out in the distance, as if in thought, then gave her gaze back to me.

"Now I wished that you were here the day I brought your gifts over."

"I know," she said. "I wished that I was here too, now."

"I just don't understand why she would do that."

"She probably kept the phone and the refill card for herself," Ronika quipped, obviously perturbed.

"Look, I'll ask her about this when I see her again," I assured Ronika. After all, I knew that a phone was there when I dropped off her gifts.

"She'll just deny it," Ronika said with conviction.

"Perhaps, but I'll ask her anyway."

Shivering slightly from the cold, I bade goodbye to Ronika and got into my car and took off. I was put off that her caregiver, a relative at that, would dictate what this teenaged girl could have. The lesson I took away from this was to make sure, in the future, that I gave every teenager their gifts in person or I'd wait until I could give it to them.

Shocked, numbed, and grieved was how I felt. How this news got by me I didn't know. But I had just been informed that Mrs. Browning succumbed to cancer over the Christmas holidays. I knew that she was gravely ill but I thought she had at least one good year left with us. But it was not to be. All of the children, with the exception of the oldest boy, who had gone off to live with his uncle down in Port Lucie, Florida, were now living with their aunt Brenda in Flagler Estates. Almost immediately, I called and offered my condolences to her and her family. She was appreciative of my call and my words of comfort and said so. I told her that I would get down there to visit her and her nieces and nephews in a day or two. She seemed pleased by that pronouncement.

That afternoon, I drove over to St Augustine Shores to pick up Erica for her counseling session. I arrived in the single family home community twenty minutes later. The property was mowed and in the middle of the lawn sat a tall cedar tree. The area near the house was landscaped with various tropical plants, including planters filled with century plants, Screw-pine, Parlor Palms, Canary Island Date Palm, Sago Palms, and Dumb Canes. On my left, in a shaded tree area, were Caladiums of various colors; pink, white, green, and red; some speckled, others veined in a contrasting color. The place was up scaled, no doubt.

I rang the doorbell and was greeted by a young freckled-faced teenager that recognized me from another visit. As I walked into a larger room to sign in, a short but stocky Black woman appeared from around the corner. Pausing, she gave me the going over. I had never seen her on my other visits.

Approaching me, she said, "And who are you?" The woman's looks and mannerisms were those you'd expect to find in a prison guard working at a state prison for women. I'm talking tough looking and hard staring.

"I'm Carl Benjamin," I answered, showing her my ID. "I'm Erica's Child Protective Services caseworker."

"How can I help you Mr. Benjamin?"

"Actually, I'm here to pick up Erica to take to her counseling session over at St Johns Mental Health Services."

"I'll get her," she said, softening her stance. "But don't forget to sign her out."

"I was in the process of doing that," I said going over to the sign in/sign out log lying on a nearby desk.

Erica looked relieved to see me when she appeared. Once we were outside I asked her how she liked it here so far.

"I love it here except for when that woman is on shift," she answered. "I don't think she likes me, or anyone else. I swear, that woman never smiles."

"Some people are like that sometimes," I said.

"Some people are like that all of the time," she came back with a chuckle.

"I can't argue with you on that," I said with a capricious smile. Entering the Cadillac, we took off for her appointment.

After I returned Erica to her group home, I headed down to the Dairy Queen just off of US1 and I-95 to conduct the James Peterson family visit.

I spied the familiar Ford van with James and his grandparents sitting inside. I parked next to them on the side of the building after filling my gas tank at the pump. Mom pulled into the parking lot five minutes later. After mom and son's loving embrace, we all entered the store, part of it Dairy Queen, the other part a gift shop. The grandparents took their usual seats a good distance away from mom and their grandson and I sat somewhere in between the two factions. While there I purchased a chili dog and fries and a drink. Later I had an ice cream cone.

An uneventful hour later, all parties parted ways and I headed home to Interlachen.

The following day I spent the better part of the morning in court. Caseworkers and court went together like tennis players and tennis courts. During court hearings, case progress was discussed and decisions were made about what parents needed to do to regain custody of their children, and whether or not they could visit with their children, whether or not a child would be sheltered, and with whom, when the children would be returned to the parent, and oftentimes, the court would decide if the children would be returned at all. My reason for being in court today was to apprise the judge of the parent's progress with their case plan and the child's progress with the services offered to them. I would also tell the judge how the child was doing in their placement and in school. This type of court hearing was known as a judicial review.

After lunch I returned to the office to work on a case plan and to organize a few case files. I was fifteen minutes into my work when I got a call from Tiffany.

"Hello, Mr. Carl, this is Tiffany."

"Hello Tiffany," I said speaking into the phone. "And how are you?"

"I'm doing fine," she replied, sounding a little tired.

"So, whatz up?" I asked. "I thought you were going to call me or stop by to let me know when I could do a home study on your new place."

"I wanted to get with you today on that but I'm still at work. My intentions were to stop by but the girl I carpool with didn't show up today," she explained, frustration evident in her voice.

"Who brought you into work?" I asked.

"My cousin had an appointment at her doctor's office so I got a ride in with her."

"So, how are you getting back to Hastings?"

"I'm hoping that someone here is going that way when we get off."

I tossed a thought or two around before asking, "What time do you get off today?"

"I get off at 4:30 this afternoon," she answered.

"Look, this is what I'll do," I said. "I have to go that way for another home visit so if you want to, I can pick you up when you get off and while we are in the area, you can show me your place and I'll do the home study then. Will that work for you?"

"Sure, that would work," she said, sounding relieved.

Reaching for my pen, I took down the directions of the assisted living facility she worked at, just off of US1, and ended my call. I returned to my paperwork. At exactly 4:30 PM, I was parked outside in the parking lot where Tiffany worked. She made an appearance shortly after my arrival.

We drove to Hastings and once there she directed me up and down streets I had never been on before. After three or four turns, along the way, we pulled into a cul-de-sac with five detached homes, two on one side and two on the other and one facing the entrance of the street. They all looked like small cottages. I could see an extension cord extending from one cottage to the one Tiffany led me inside of.

The place was pretty decent. It had been remodeled but it was evident that more work needed to be done before anyone moved in. As for size, it wasn't a large place but she had little ones anyway. No, I saw had no issue with the size of the home. But this thing about the extension cord providing electricity from the adjacent cottage wasn't going to fly and I told her so.

She said it was a temporary connection until she could get an electrician out to do some electric work. Right then I told her that once the electrical work was done and certified safe by an inspector, call me and we would get together and do the home study then. She seemed to be all right with that. She asked me to drop her off at her mother's house when I left.

Heading south, I made my way to Flagler Estates to visit with the Browning siblings and their aunt Brenda.

Chapter 16

As much as I worked in and around historic St Augustine, I rarely was afforded the opportunity to play tourist. I did that Saturday. There was a Red Lobster that Cynthia loved to dine at near my agency in St Augustine but this time I managed to convince her to dine with me at Scarlett O'Hara's in the historic area of town. It was a popular restaurant with a covered porch and had good food. I loved their barbeque spareribs. Parking was a challenge for most people but I knew a place to park that was only three blocks away in an area that did not have any parking meters.

I parked the Cadillac in my usual curbside spot under a large oak tree adjacent to several bungalows and a church and Cynthia and I walked, hand in hand, the three blocks to the restaurant, just across from Flagler College, a campus that used to be a resort hotel for the rich and famous back in the 30s and 40s.

For the next three hours the two of us dined and strolled along St George Street. It was a beautiful day. Actually, it was a lovely day. And the two of us were having the time of our lives. I had not felt this way in a long time but it was a memory worth revisiting. After we bought ice cream cones at one of our favorite spots, we walked over to the Casa Monica Hotel where we rested for a short while in the lobby before heading back to my car. We took off after that to head over the Bridge of Lions and onto the beach. For an hour that evening, we strolled along the sandy shoreline as the sun lowered itself in the sly overhead. At one point, by a one of many support pillars under a pier, I took her magnificent form into my embrace and kissed her long and hard. It was only our second time kissing and I found myself having to steady myself, after taking a deep breath, and exhaling. Kissing her left me wonderfully dazed.

Looking into her enchanting eyes and bright smile, I professed to her that I was falling in love with her. That's when she told me that she had been in love with me since the day she first laid eyes on me. With our hearts beating wildly, we kissed again and again. I almost forgot where I was and frankly, I didn't care. But she tempered my passion by saying that she thought we ought to be heading back to the car and onto Palatka before we were charged with indecent behavior in a public setting. We both broke out laughing as we made our way back to the car.

We returned to her place and talked for a short while. God, I was feeling on top of the world. The feelings I had were up there with winning the lotto. We were kissing when my cellphone rang. It was my mother. She had called to let me know that a good friend of the family had died in a car accident. Numbed, I ended the call. I gave Cynthia a solemn gaze and told her what had happened back in Philadelphia and said that I was going to head back home. I knew that I wasn't going to be my ole bubbly self after hearing this tragic news. Cynthia asked me if I wanted her to tag along and I told her that I'd be all right, that there was no need for her to drive that distance when I wasn't going to be good company anyway. The family friend had been shot to death by her estranged husband. Some people are born sore losers.

Everyone had been holding their breath wondering how long Dennis would last in his current placement. It was less than two months. His foster care mother had tolerated as much as she could during his stay there but she drew the line when he began to break up her precious furniture and valuable collectibles.

After he was dismissed from school I picked him up at the house, along with all of his personal belongings, which amounted to two large trash bags and two pairs of shoes. He was being moved into a therapeutic foster care group home for boys. Actually the home I just took him from was only a temporary placement. The therapeutic group home was something the agency had been working on for months to get this kid into. Ironically, he was going to be moved there the following week anyway but with this incident, it was decided to fast track the boy's entry.

After a staff member and I got Dennis settled in at his new group home, I returned to the main office to finish filling out paperwork. At one point in the process, I paused to read a notation in his record which read: ADHD/Conduct Disorder and Severe Intermittent Explosive Disorder/Antisocial Traits. Meds: Seroquel 25mg twice daily /Adderall 30mg once daily / Depakote 125mg twice daily. And this boy was just six years old, I'm thinking.

When I returned to the office, Dennis's grandmother, Darlene Sawgrass, was waiting for me in the lobby. She had been cleared to have supervised visits with Amber's children by the court the week before.

"How can I help you Mrs. Sawgrass?" I asked approaching her where she was had been sitting but was now standing.

"I just stopped by to see when I could get to visit with Dennis, whom she referred to as Denny, and the other children," she answered, the wrinkles in her forehead apparent. "As you know, the judge granted me supervised visits."

"That's right, and I know you are anxious to see them," I replied, shaking her hand. "I just got through moving Dennis into a new group home."

Mrs. Sawgrass gave me an odd look. "Denny's been moved again?"

"He wore out his welcome, you might say."

"Where is he at now?" she asked.

"If you don't mind coming with me to my office, I'll write the phone number and address down on a piece of paper for you," I said.

"No, I don't mind at all," she said.

We entered my office, rather very small cubicle, and once I found the information, I jotted it down for her.

"Please make sure you call them and make arrangements for a visit with him before just showing up there," I cautioned her.

"I will, Mr. Carl," she assured me.

With our business now completed, I escorted her back to the main lobby. Returning to my desk, I sat down to organize a number of files. I had a case review scheduled in a few days with my acting supervisor and I wanted to be ready for it.

That evening I headed up to Middleburg, Florida to visit Vanessa, the lovely one year old angel in Kevin's caseload who was born with an undeveloped brain. This was a case where the parents were never involved in the child's life.

Vanessa was lying in her crib but was wide awaked, or at least she looked as though she was gazing about her surroundings when I arrived. However, the foster care mother said that though she looked normal and acted normal, she was not conscious of what was going on around her. In a sense, Vanessa was practically brain dead, I was told, though very much alive.

As on my previous visit, I asked to pick Vanessa up and hold her in my arms. Today she had on a yellow outfit and was wearing matching yellow socks. Her hazel brown eyes surveyed me but never once did she respond to my gaze and my baby talk. Like the foster mom warned me she would, she looked at me and through me as if I wasn't there. I kissed her on the forehead and said another silent prayer, then laid her back down in her crib.

Misty eyed and chocked up, I left shortly after my thirty minute visit and headed home to Interlachen.

The following morning I found myself back at the hospital with Erica. She said she was still experiencing pain in her stomach area and felt there was something more going on than a yeast infection. She occupied the same chair next to where I sat on our last visit and assumed the same slouched down position as before. After her vitals were taken, I trained my attention on the morning news show while we waited to be called to see the doctor. And we were, some forty-five minutes later.

Unlike before, this time they ordered a battery of tests for her which prolonged our visit there by four hours. At one point they put her in a room, and in bed, in the ER area that had a bed and television and a bathroom. I was beginning to wonder if they were going to admit her. When they dropped off a tray of food for her lunch in bed, I walked over to the cafeteria to have lunch. When I returned, she was asleep so I took a seat on a chair in the room and watched television while we waited.

After the results of her last test had been reviewed by the doctor, two hours later, he came in to talk to both of us. Whatever was bothering Erica and causing her pain, they could not find the source of it. I was glad that there was nothing seriously wrong with her but I was puzzled about what might have caused her pain. I did not think that she had made any of this up. Doctors do overlook things, I told her after the physician had left the room. Why it took nearly five hours to figure this out I could not fathom.

After she dressed, we headed out. I stopped at the office first to check on a few things and to give my supervisor, and the program manager, an update. They gave me a puzzled look when I told them that the doctor could find nothing wrong with Erica. They asked me if she could have been putting on just to get out of school. I told them that I didn't think that was the case but I could have been wrong. My philosophy was always to give the child the benefit of the doubt, until I was proven absolutely wrong. Even the doctor had said that it could be something they've missed.

I returned Erica to her foster care home and headed out for a few home visits. It had been a long day and I was ready to call it an early night once I got home. Once I arrived there, I ate, watched a movie, showered, shaved, and swabbed my face with a piping hot washcloth. Going into my bedroom, I called it a day

By the end of the week, one of our caseworkers was fired. The reasons why were never revealed officially but unofficially, the rumor mill reported that she had not been doing her home visits as she should have been doing. She'd go there to the house but never inside. She'd talk to the caregivers at the door, ask them if everything was alright, had them sign her home visit form, then would take off. One too many caregivers began to call in about her brief encounters with them. And there was an abundance of paperwork that she was behind on, as well. As always, when someone was let go, we would all be told to meet in our tight and cramped cubicle area the following morning for an important announcement where Karen, our program manager, would tell us who had been let go but never why, which I understood. Also by the end of the week, I got a call from Ronika's aunt telling me that she had moved to Palm Coast and that she needed a home study done by me.

The first thing I did after lunch was to gather my home study paperwork. I also updated the new address information on the computer. Signing out, I took off for Palm Coast.

It was a beautiful stone built house and the interior was much more spacious and brighter than the small house she had moved from in Palatka, Florida. As she had done in her former home, Wanda started up a licensed daycare business out of her new home. There were three cribs with newborns sleeping inside of and two little toddlers there watching television, both too young to attend any preschool programs.

"So, what do you think of my new house?" she asked, giving me a guided tour.

"It's lovely," I said, taking it all in.

As we walked about she went on to tell me about her plans for this room and that room and this space and that space and what kind of furniture she had in mind to place here and over there. She had done well investing the insurance money from her husband's death. She was all business and you might say quite ambitious, at least her plans were. But I admired that part of her. Some spouses would have squandered the life insurance money.

Before leaving, I reminded her to have Ronika's school records transferred from Palatka High School to Flagler/Palm Coast High School. After I completed my home study, I departed. Wanting to visit with Ronika before I left the area, I drove over to her school to visit with her. That way, I would not have to make a separate trip back to Palm Coast just to see her.

When I first met Ronika she seemed to have an innocence and vulnerability about her, much like a child, but now she was beginning to look like, act like, and dress like a young lady. You see, once you work with a child long enough in this business, you get to see some of them grow up, some for the better and some for the worst.

Quiet and reserved by nature, her level of maturity spoke volumes. She was getting good grades in school, getting along a lot better with her aunt, for now, and was learning how to drive, she had told me in an earlier conversation over the phone. All in all, I saw in this young girl someone who was preparing herself for life after eighteen, a life on her own.

"Hello Ronika," I said in greeting after she was escorted into the conference room by a young office aide.

"Hello Carl," she said beaming. "You came all of the way down to Palm Coast just to see me?" she asked incredulously, her voice rising as she took a seat across from me.

"Well, that and the fact that I needed to conduct a home study on your aunt's new house," I answered leaning back in the chair.

"I guess she's still at the house with the kids babysitting."

"She was when I left," I said. "So, how do you like your new school?"

"I like it," she said without any expression. "But I still miss all of my friends back at Palatka High."

"You'll meet new people here," I assured her. "It always works out like that."

"Well there is this one boy I think likes me in my fourth period class," she said.

I raised an eyebrow feinting parental concern. "Now, now, you can't be too careful about these things Ronika. Boys are nothing but trouble. They're lazy, irresponsible, immature, adventurous, unstable, unreliable, and sometime West Side Story delinquent. By the time I finished she looked taken aback. That's when I leaned forward and smiled and said, "Gotcha!"

Now amused, she broke into a smile and rapped me playfully on the forearm with her closed fist. "You know, you were beginning to sound like a parent there for a second," she said.

"Look, it sounds like you really like this boy," I said with a toothy smile.

"He's alright," she said though not fooling me.

"And what about your boyfriend, the one whose mother has a beauty care store in East Palatka?" I asked.

"We're still seeing each other," she confessed. "But it's always good to have a little something to fall back on."

We both smiled.

"Look, I'm leaving that one alone. Just remember why you are here and that is to get an education," I reminded her. "Get that and you'll have plenty of time for boys later on."

I left the school shortly after that conversation. I believed she appreciated the fact that I had responded, though in jest, like the parent she never really had. You see, I thoroughly understood that none of the children in foster care or a relative or non-relative placement, with the exception of those whose parents were deceased or medically unable to care for them, would be where they were now if their parents were productive and active participants in their lives,. I got that message. Some workers did not, nor did they seem to care.

Mondays were days you could never know what to expect in this business, being that it was the first day back to work. Things happen on the weekend that you do not usually find out about until Monday morning. Well, over the weekend, we had a young foster care girl die in the hospital. She had been ill for some time now and had taken a turn for the worst. I knew not the girl or the particulars of her case but her caseworker appeared pretty distraught and so did a few others involved in the case. For the rest of us, it was a gloomy Monday.

Later in the day I got a frantic call from Roxanne. Aaron had gone to trial the week before and on Friday was sentenced to three years in prison for assault with a deadly weapon and for being a felon found in the possession of a gun. Roxanne was panicky and unsure how she would survive without Aaron. I told her she might want to start looking for a job, since I knew she was not working and had not worked in years. She said she did not know where to start looking for a job or how to go about doing the paperwork. I told her she could start at the employment center within walking distance of my job, that is, if she could get over to my office. I said that I would go over to the job center if she felt she needed moral support and encouragement. That's when she said that she had no way to get over to my office.

"This is what I can do, Roxanne," I said into the phone. "I can pick you up after lunch and take you over to the job center and see how they could assist you."

"That will be fine," she replied. "I really would appreciate that."

"Good. Then I'll see you around 1:30 this afternoon."

"Yes, see you then," she said.

I hung up the phone but the impression I was left with was that Roxanne was not at all excited about looking for work. Yes, I was going to get her to the place but from that point on, she would have to take the ball and run with it, figuratively speaking. For the same reason why I was going out of my way to assist her, because of her little one and because she was pregnant, she would have to use that same line of reasoning for getting a job.

I picked her up shortly after lunch. She was wearing a light colored blouse and Daisy Duke cutoff shorts. It wasn't the kind of attire you'd expect one to wear going to a job center, even if it was for information. But that's what she was wearing and I did not have time to wait for her to change. That would have tacked on another thirty minutes.

"So, have you heard from Aaron since he was taken into custody?" I said as I cut across the silence that prevailed.

"He called me last night and we talked briefly," she said peering over at me. "I am so worried. I just don't know how I'm going to make it for the next three years, Carl."

"Well that's one reason why we're going over to the job center now," I said as I came to a stop at a red light.

"God, I haven't been in the work force for over two years," she said, looking out the window on her side. "And things have changed, I'm sure."

"That is a long time," I said as the light turned green and I drove on. "And things do change. What kind of work did you do when you were working?"

"I did some waitressing."

"Why did you stop?"

"I got pregnant."

"I see," I murmured. "Did you finish high school?"

"No, I dropped out in eleventh grade," she answered. "I regret having done that now."

"You plan on getting a GED?"

"I need to," she quipped.

"But are you planning on getting it?" I reemphasized.

"I haven't really given it a lot of thought," she said.

"Roxanne," I began. "You really ought to seriously start thinking about getting yourself in a position where you don't have to rely on Aaron, the government, or anybody else, for that matter."

"I know and I need to."

"Then think about going back to school to get yourself some education. Do it for your children, if nothing else," I ended.

We arrived at the job center less than twenty minutes later. It was located within walking distance of my job. We exited my car. She asked if she could take a quick smoke before we went in. Since she seemed a little edgy, I agreed to wait on her for a quick smoke. Once she had stamped out the butt of the cigarette, we went inside the job center where we were helped after a ten minute wait.

I did not go back with her because there were some things she needed to learn to do on her own initiative. I was there primarily to provide her transportation and motivation. Roxanne needed money, her own place, and she needed a job. She also needed to work on her self-esteem. She was far too dependent on others. Currently she was staying with a girlfriend of hers while her son was still in the care of her own mother. When I went to pick her up earlier, the place inside reeked of incense. I asked her, once she had gotten into the car, why the couple she was staying with burned incense and she nervously replied that they just happened to love the fragrance it produced and that it had nothing to do with smoking marijuana. I never mentioned pot but she obviously knew where I was going with my line of questioning.

Twenty minutes later, she reappeared from the job counselor's office with a handful of forms. We left the premises shortly after that. As we drove off she began to tell me what she had found out and what she told them she was interested in.

"Did they have many full time jobs to offer, the kind with benefits?" I asked.

Looking over at me, she bit her lip, and as plainly as I had ever heard anyone speak, she said, "Oh, I told them that I was only interested in part time jobs."

So much with being there to motivate her, I told myself.

Chapter 17

Penny stopped by after a hiatus of nearly two months to let me know that she was still alive, if not completely well. She told me she had gone off to Georgia with some friends to find work, or so she claimed, and while up there got into a bad accident and was hospitalized for a couple of days. She said she had injured her arm real bad but was all right overall. I reminded her that she had two little boys, one old enough to verbal say he missed her being around, and needed to get serious about completing her case plan. I told her that she needed to start thinking about their future and her own. I ended by telling her it took a mature mind to settle down and do the right thing. She agreed with me and took my mild chiding for what it was...a nugget of wisdom.

Another lost parent made an unexpected appearance by phone. It was Alisha, mother of the twins, little Shannon, and John. She was calling to say that she had returned from her hiatus in Texas and was ready to complete her case plan and regain custody of her children. I encouraged her to do just that.

Darlene Sawgrass, maternal grandmother of Dennis and Deidra and Deon stopped by to say that she had gotten around to visiting with Dennis but now wanted to set up a visit with the younger two children. By now, their mother Amber was back in jail in St Johns County for VOP. Because she had cases in three counties, once she was violated in one, she was violated in all three. That meant, once she served time in one, she would be transported to the next to serve time there, then after that, she would be transferred again to the third jail to serve her time out there before being released. Don Juan Elders, the legal father of Deidra and the biological father of Deon, was also incarcerated in St Johns County Jail for VOP.

I told her that since I was scheduled to visit with the two younger children that afternoon, I could meet her at a playground near the new parking garage in the historic district and we could turn my visit into a family visit. And because the playground was a few blocks from where Dennis was staying at, I could pick him up as well and bring him along for the visit. Grandma was ecstatic. She asked me what time to be there and after I told her, we both parted company.

That afternoon, I picked up the Elder children and then Dennis and drove over to the playground. The menace actual behaved civilly around his younger siblings. Darlene arrived a few minutes after our arrival. For an hour she enjoyed the company of her grands. She had even brought along some cookies and ice cream for them, along with paper plates and plastic spoons. For the next couple of weeks we met here and the children got to visit with a relative, though their parents seemed to be out of the picture by now.

Over a month later Darlene's probation was violated on account of driving with a suspended license and with cannabis in her system. That ended the weekly family visits. As much as Dennis was a screwed up child, I could see why in some ways. The entire family appeared to be dysfunctional.

The following day I attended an ESI staffing. The case centered on a sixteen year old male named Oliver Anderson. I had read the case file the evening before. It was said that the child had been placed with the maternal grandmother, due to inadequate shelter, food and supervision on the part of the child's father, and the child's mother's pronounced absence from his life. This proceeding originated out of a Putnam County Dependency case. Over a period of time the grandmother's mental capacity came into question, as well as her behavior. It was now believed that grandma was suffering from Alzheimer's disease. Under her supervision and care, she had become verbally and physically abusive with Oliver. The child expressed that he was often cursed out and hit repeatedly by his grandmother for reasons he often did not know. He loved his grandmother but thought she needed help.

When questioned, his mother, Yvette Trumble, claimed that she had similar run-ins with her mother. They would get into arguments for no apparent reasons and then her mother would cuss her out, telling her to get off of her property. The mother said she could no longer take it and left, although her son remained. The child's father stated that he was unable to care for the boy due to his poor health. Oliver did get about $27 a month from his father's Social Security funds.

Once Oliver was removed from his grandmother's care, he was placed with Alexandria and Eugene Copeland, the parents of his best friend, who lived in Fruit Cove, Florida. Fruit Cove was a pretty affluent area with homes that ranged in the lower 80s up to a couple of millions of dollars. It was about a forty-five minute drive, pre-rush hour, from the office. Because of his father's poor health, and his mother's inability to raise him, the placement was one of permanency.

Oliver loved playing basketball and so did his best friend. When I first visited the house and drove up into the long driveway, one reminisce of an Italian home in Italy with tall Palm trees and large Sega Palms and a circular driveway, I thought I was meeting a banker type, meaning white family. I was pleasantly surprised to find out that the tenants, rather owners, were a Black family. I had been visiting this area for years when I visited my computer cohort and friend Jim Messick, who lived less than a mile away, and never saw any Black families. But the couple told me that they had lived there for the past sixteen years. I wasn't sure about Eugene Copeland but his lovely wife, Alexandria, was from the island of Antiqua. Both the husband and wife told me they were prior navy. Retired from the service, he now worked for the United Parcel Service, which was better known as UPS.

The case was one of my most involved cases and at times, emotionally draining. I knew that the Copeland's were doing their best to help Oliver and they had gone out of their way to pay for his school trips, whatever activity that involved basketball, including summer training, and all without any financial assistance from the state. And they still had their own son to pay for these activities. Yet, Oliver seemed unappreciative at times. There were days he grew lazy and times when he grew arrogant and you don't do that in anyone else's home, especially when they're taking care of you. Several times I was called over by Alexandria to mediate a crisis there at the home. Those were the times Eugene had said he had had enough and that Oliver had to go. I understood his anger and frustration but I could also see that it was affecting their relationship. You see, as much as Oliver was acting contrary, she went to bat for him when her husband put down his foot and said that he had to go. Many times I sat down at the table with them, both indoors and outdoors on the patio, and watch both parents press their case with teary eyes. Twice I confronted Oliver and twice he was close to breaking down, as he promised the world to be able to stay in their home and not be put out.

After our mediations, many times with moist eyes myself, Eugene would relinquish and allow the boy another reprieve and a chance to prove him wrong. But he was adamant that Oliver would find a way to screw things up again. Actually, I understood and sympathized with both non-relative parents' viewpoints and I was just as torn about the situation as they were. Fortunately, when Oliver lived up to his expectations and responsibilities, the placement went well. I was thankful for that. But far too often, it was touch and go with that placement.

Two months later, the world was a lot different in many ways. On a personal level, Cynthia and I were now engaged though there wasn't a set date for the wedding. As for my clients, my client Alisha, mother of the twins, had gotten back with Jeremy Jameson, her estranged but patient husband, and completed her case plan and had found a house to rent. Having done these things, the court granted her custody of her children. Alyson and her son Sergio moved into a new apartment complex after she completed her nurse assistants' training and Tiffany got that electrical problem solved at her cottage and was eventually granted full custody of her three children. As for the Browning children, six of the seven were still living and thriving with their aunt Brenda and her husband and their two children in their five bedroom manufactured home in Flagler Estates. The oldest child, Frederick, who had gone to south Florida to live with his favorite uncle months earlier, found himself in serious trouble as a result of getting caught up with the wrong crowd. As part of a three man burglary team, he was sentenced to twenty years minimum in a state prison for breaking into a residence that involved a deadly shooting. Some adolescents, like some adults, just never learn.

In Middleburg, Florida, little Vanessa was still clinging onto life, a life she had no sensory perception of. Only God Almighty knew where her thoughts were at any given time, that is, if she had any thoughts at all. The doctors didn't think she did. And Ronika went on to finish eleventh grade with above average grades. Her aunt's daughter did not fare as well. While Ronika was promoted, her cousin was left behind a grade.

Little six year old, Dennis the menace, was still living out his preteen years in a therapeutic foster care group home and probably would be there until he turned 18 years of age. James Peterson remained in the care of his paternal grandparents, Fred and Harriett. Mom had yet to complete her case plan and I wasn't sure if she ever would. Elyse's two beautiful girls' temporary non-relative placement was turned into a permanent non-relative placement when mom failed to complete her case plan after a year's time. Mom just could not stay away from drugs and no good men.

Erica remained in foster care and was certain to remain there until she turned eighteen. She still complained about her stomach. Though abandoned by her parents, she maintained a positive outlook on life. As for Penny, she was still out there trying to find herself and her place in life. I only wished that she would have found time and a place in her heart for her two boys, one who desperately missed his mother. But Penny seemed to be searching for something and I wasn't sure she would ever find what she was looking for. Sadly, in her search for fulfillment, she managed to overlook the three most important people in her life, her two boys and her aunt, all whom loved and cared for her.

There had also been additions to the staff and a few purges, as well. People in this line of work rarely stayed in it more than five or six years. It was that demanding and that emotionally draining. Those who remained longer than six years had found a way to shield themselves from the day to day office drama, the courtroom drama, and the drama that came with interacting with emotionally charged parents and defiant children. Most of these children were damaged goods when they arrived on our doorsteps, but ninety percent of them were savable given the right opportunities and the right services and the right caseworker. Unfortunately, the state hires just about anyone with a degree to do this job and the training they receive rarely touches upon actually situations a caseworker may find himself or herself facing once out of the classroom. And Lord help you if you make the wrong decision because the system is unforgiving.

Then there's always the possibility you might lose a child. It does happen. It never happened to anyone in my caseload but it has happened to a few of my caseworkers. Nothing hits you harder in the solar plexus than the death of one of your children. It hurts beyond expressed words. In the end, you just hope that you had no culpability in their demise. You see, when things like that happened, every visit you made was scrutinized and every detail of the case you were involved with was held under a microscope. This business doesn't get any more high profile than when a child dies while in the care of the state.

Contrary to what my ex-fiancée thought about my job, I knew it was an important job and the manner in which I approached it was with circumspection. You see, I wanted to be the kind of caseworker I'd want to have if I was a child placed in the system; a child away from loved ones and away from any semblance of a loving, caring, and stable life. I understand one has to be detached to some degree but far too many caseworkers translate this into meaning no attachments at all. Children are keen and can tell if you really are invested in them or just doing your job. The way I looked at it, my job went beyond paperwork and courtroom hearings and staffings. I made it my job to have a positive impact on the children assigned to me, those who could be impacted. We were dealing with and interacting with other human beings, not cattle, or just another case. With me, it was never about being just another case. Sadly, it's that way with some caseworkers, many who are turning off the very children they are supposed to be helping. Fortunately, there were a lot more good case workers than they were bad caseworkers. Me, I didn't want to be a bad caseworker and it was hard for me to define what a really good caseworker was, so I went out of my way to be an effective caseworker. In all honesty, I didn't know how to do this job any other way.

Easing back an inch or two in my office chair, I put away all of my case files in my file drawer and tidied up my desk and cubicle area. I was about to leave for the day when Karen, our program manager, asked me if I had a minute. I told her certainly. Though we talked after work on occasion, it was far and between when we did. Usually, whenever I was about to pass her office on the way out at the end of the day, I'd spy her at her desk and stop in. That's when we would sit down and talk about matters that concerned the job and things that had little to do with the job.

The times she personally summoned me to her office, was usually the times she wanted to go over something with me that was job related. So that was my frame of mind as I followed her. This being business, now what? I thought.

Once inside of her office, she sat down at her desk and leaned back. She signaled for me to sit down as well.

"So, how's everything going with you, Carl?"

"Fine," I said, still wondering if this was official business or a social call.

"Is your ex fiancée still up in Alaska visiting her son?" she asked, leaning back in her chair.

"Naah, I think she's in Philly."

"You two plan on getting back together anytime soon?"

"I don't think so," I answered as Renée's face flashed across my mind. "I tried to work things out with her and get her to reconsider but I don't think she wanted to reconcile," I said coyly but frankly.

"That must have been tough on you," she said, her piercing eyes trained on my eyes.

"It was for a while but I should have told you that I am engaged to another beautiful young lady," I said to her surprise.

"Get out of here! I didn't know that Carl," she said leaning forward. "Congratulations! I'm telling you, you-are-so-private."

"When I'm here, I'm usually focused on my work, Karen," I explained. "But thanks for the congratulations."

"Anyway, you probably think this was a social call. Well it is, sort of, but I have some more good news for you. Are you interested in hearing it?"

"Sure, why not," I answered my curiosity really piqued now.

"You know that Russ is no longer with us, right?"

"Yes, I know."

"Well, I want you to fill his spot."

"You want me to fill his spot," I repeated, not believing my ears.

"Yes, I want you to be my next supervisor."

"Do I have a choice?" I smiled.

"Nope," she chuckled. "Are you interested?"

"Of course, I am," I said breaking into a bigger smile.

"Then consider the job yours," she said.

"Alright!" I railed.

I thanked her profusely, then we got down to the real important stuff, my salary. When all was said and done, I left her office with five thousand dollar raise. It was going to be goodbye cubicle and goodbye caseload. Supervisors did not carry caseloads. They monitored them and they reviewed them.

As happy as I was when I left Karen's office, I knew that my new positioned carried with it a lot of responsibilities. But I was prepared to give it my all. On a more sober note, it meant that I would no longer be on the beat, meaning dealing directly with children, which I loved to do and where I felt I had the greatest impact on their lives. Now I was going to be a manager and as great as that sounded, I think I was born to be a caseworker.

Walking back into the empty cubicle room I stood quietly in front of my desk. Tomorrow I would move into a new office of my own, as well as into a new job position. For that moment, I savored the memories I had had as a caseworker. Things just were not going to be the same, from this point on, I told myself. It was one thing to be responsible for your actions to an organization. It was an entirely different thing to be responsible for other people's actions. Their screw ups and oversights could turn out to be career ending, mine included. But I was ready to give it a try.

This was not my first time up at bat in a management position, far from it. But this position involved the lives of children left in the hands and care of the people I was responsible for. That was something I had to think about and I did before I ever said yes to Karen. Time would tell if this was what I really wanted to do, I told myself.

On the way out, I passed by Elizabeth's office to see if she was in. I wanted something sweet to munch on but the door was locked. She had been my main source for candy.

Across from her office was the Independent Living office. Glancing inside, I spied Rory, one of the Independent Living counselors, and I spied a bowl of candy. I asked him if I could treat myself to their candy dish. He smiled and told me to go right ahead.

Entering the room, I selected two mini chocolate Hershey's from the candy dish, said goodbye to Rory, turned, and walked out of the building for the last time as a caseworker. Once outside, I made a beeline to my Cadillac which was parked a short distance away.

After I drove off, I called Cynthia to tell her the good news and to let her know to get ready to go out. Tonight it was going to be dinner for two with my fiancée at Chili's Restaurant in Palatka, Florida, another favorite place we loved to dine at. For this one night, I was going to eat at the upper management salary level, dessert and all. As they say in France...bon appetite!

www.ingramcontent.com/pod-product-compliance
Lightning Source LLC
Chambersburg PA
CBHW081109290526
45795CB00006B/2052